OECD Development Co-operation Peer Reviews: Portugal 2016

Please cite this publication as:
OECD (2015), *OECD Development Co-operation Peer Reviews: Portugal 2016*, OECD Publishing, Paris.
http://dx.doi.org/10.1787/9789264248571-en

ISBN 978-92-64-24856-4 (print)
ISBN 978-92-64-24857-1 (PDF)

Series: OECD Development Co-operation Peer Reviews
ISSN 2309-7124 (print)
ISSN 2309-7132 (online)

Corrigenda to OECD publications may be found on line at: *www.oecd.org/about/publishing/corrigenda.htm*.

Conducting the peer review

The OECD Development Assistance Committee (DAC) conducts periodic reviews of the individual development co-operation efforts of DAC members. The policies and programmes of each member are critically examined approximately once every four or five years. Five members are examined annually. The OECD Development Co-operation Directorate provides analytical support, and develops and maintains, in close consultation with the Committee, the methodology and analytical framework – known as the Reference Guide – within which the peer reviews are undertaken.

The objectives of DAC peer reviews are to improve the quality and effectiveness of development co-operation policies and systems, and to promote good development partnerships for better impact on poverty reduction and sustainable development in developing countries. DAC peer reviews assess the performance of a given member, not just that of its development co-operation agency, and examine both policy and implementation. They take an integrated, system-wide perspective on the development co-operation and humanitarian assistance activities of the member under review.

The peer review is prepared by a team, consisting of representatives of the Secretariat working with officials from two DAC members who are designated as "examiners". The country under review provides a memorandum setting out the main developments in its policies and programmes. Then the Secretariat and the examiners visit the capital to interview officials, parliamentarians, as well as civil society and NGO representatives of the donor country to obtain a first-hand insight into current issues surrounding the development co-operation efforts of the member concerned. Field visits assess how members are implementing the major DAC policies, principles and concerns, and review operations in recipient countries, particularly with regard to poverty reduction, sustainability, gender equality and other aspects of participatory development, and local aid co-ordination. During the field visit, the team meets with representatives of the partner country's administration, parliamentarians, civil society and other development partners. For this peer review, the team visited Sao Tome and Principe.

The Secretariat then prepares a draft report on the member's development co-operation which is the basis for the DAC review meeting at the OECD. At this meeting senior officials from the member under review respond to questions formulated by the Committee in association with the examiners.

This review contains the main findings and recommendations of the Development Assistance Committee and the report of the Secretariat. It was prepared with examiners from the Czech Republic and Luxembourg for the Peer Review of Portugal on 10 November 2015.

Table of contents

Tables

Figures

Boxes

Abbreviations and acronyms

Camões, I.P.	Camões Cooperation and Language Institute
CERF	Central Emergency Response Fund
CGD	Center for Global Development
COHAFA	Committee on Humanitarian Aid and Food Aid
COP	Conference of State Parties
CPLP	Community of Portuguese Speaking Countries
CSO	Civil society organisation
DAC	Development Assistance Committee
ECDPM	European Centre for Development Policy Management
ECHO	European Commission Humanitarian Office
EU	European Union
GHD	Good Humanitarian Donorship
GNI	Gross national income
GOP	Government of Portugal
IASC	Inter-Agency Steering Committee
IATI	International Aid Transparency Initiative
ICP	Indicative Cooperation Programme
IPAD	Instituto Português de Apoio ao Desenvolvimento
ISO	International Organization for Standardization
LDC	Least developed country
MNE	Ministério dos Negócios Estrangeiros
NGO	Non-governmental organisation
OCHA	United Nations Office for the Coordination of Humanitarian Affairs
ODA	Official Development Assistance
OECD	Organisation for Economic Co-operation and Development
PALOP	Portuguese-speaking African countries
SIDS	Small island developing states
SOFID	Sociedade para o Financiamento do Desenvolvimento
STP	Sao Tome and Principe
UN	United Nations
UNDP	United Nations Development Programme
UNICEF	United Nations Children's Fund
UNFPA	United Nations Population Fund
UNODC	United Nations Office on Drugs and Crime

Signs used:

EUR	Euros
USD	United States dollars
( )	Secretariat estimate in whole or part
-	Nil
0.0	Negligible
..	Not available
...	Not available separately, but included in total
n.a.	Non applicable

Slight discrepancies in totals are due to rounding.

Annual average exchange rates (EUR for USD) were:

2009	2010	2011	2012	2013
0.7181	0.7550	0.7192	0.7780	0.7532

Portugal's aid at a glance

PORTUGAL

Gross Bilateral ODA, 2012-13 average, unless otherwise shown

Net ODA	2012	2013	Change 2012/13
Current (USD m)	581	488	-15.9%
Constant (2012 USD m)	581	466	-19.7%
In Euro (million)	452	368	-18.6%
ODA/GNI	0.28%	0.23%	
Bilateral share	68%	62%	

Top Ten Recipients of Gross ODA (USD million)	
1 Cabo Verde	166
2 Mozambique	82
3 Morocco	29
4 Angola	24
5 Sao Tome and Principe	19
6 Timor-Leste	19
7 China (People's Republic of)	11
8 Guinea-Bissau	9
9 Brazil	6
10 Afghanistan	1
Memo: Share of gross bilateral ODA	
Top 5 recipients	82%
Top 10 recipients	94%
Top 20 recipients	95%

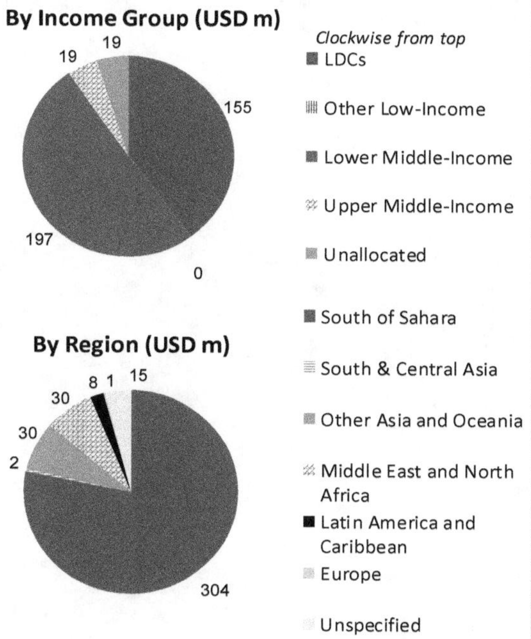

By Income Group (USD m)
19
19
155
197
0
Clockwise from top
LDCs
Other Low-Income
Lower Middle-Income
Upper Middle-Income
Unallocated
By Region (USD m)
8 1 15
30
30
2
304
South of Sahara
South & Central Asia
Other Asia and Oceania
Middle East and North Africa
Latin America and Caribbean
Europe
Unspecified

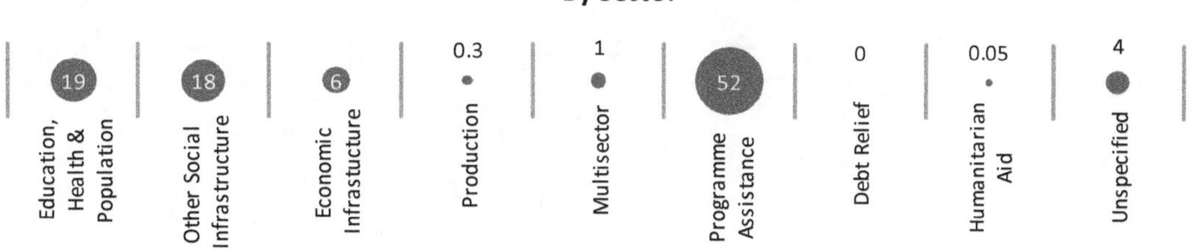

By Sector
19
Education, Health & Population
18
Other Social Infrastructure
6
Economic Infrastucture
0.3
Production
1
Multisector
52
Programme Assistance
0
Debt Relief
0.05
Humanitarian Aid
4
Unspecified

Figure 0.1 Portugal's implementation of the 2010 peer review recommendations

Not examined: 1 (5%)
Implemented: 5 (25%)
Partially implemented: 8 (40%)
Not implemented: 6 (30%)

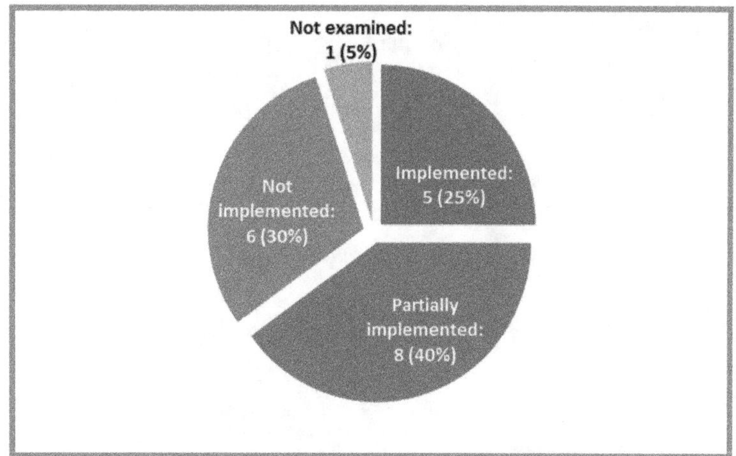

Context of Portugal's peer review

Since 2010 Portugal has faced a severe economic crisis, which has resulted in considerable fiscal consolidation and has affected all parts of the Portuguese economy and society. This DAC peer review of Portugal's development co-operation takes place as the country is starting to show signs of recovery, though still facing significant challenges. Portugal submitted to an Economic and Financial Assistance Programme with the European Union and the International Monetary Fund between May 2011 and June 2014. Wide-ranging structural reforms and fiscal consolidation brought by the programme have started to help the economy return to modest growth, with GDP projected to reach 1.5% in 2015. Competitiveness is improving, and export performance has risen. However, unemployment, while declining, remains high at 13.9%, investment has plummeted, and external debt levels remain elevated.

The Portuguese government has brought down its deficit from -11.2% of GDP in 2010 to -4.9% in 2014. A more modest pace of government consolidation is envisaged in the coming year, with Portugal's 2015 budget aiming to bring the deficit in line with Europe's "fiscal compact", or within -3% of GDP.

Portugal's significant public sector reform programme has been guided by its Plan for Reduction and Improvement of Public Administration (PREMAC). Overall public sector employment has fallen by 8% since the beginning of 2012, and public sector wage costs have been reduced.

As part of this public sector reform process, Portugal merged its development agency in 2012 – IPAD – with its culture and language institute – Camões Institute. The new institute, Camões I.P., has a mandate for development co-operation, culture and language promotion. It reports to two Secretaries of State within the Ministry of Foreign Affairs and has separate budgets and organisational units for its different roles, with a shared management and administrative structure. The merger was aimed primarily at achieving efficiencies and could also enhance Portugal's development co-operation impact due to the opportunity for increased synergies.

As of 2011, Portugal has been governed by a centre-right coalition of the Social Democratic Party and the small, conservative Popular Party. Elections are planned for October 2015 with a Presidential election scheduled for January 2016.

Sources:

EIU (2015), *Country Report Portugal,* July 2015, EIU (Economist Intelligence Unit), London.

OECD (2014a), *OECD Economic Surveys: Portugal 2014*, OECD Publishing, Paris, http://dx.doi.org/10.1787/eco_surveys-prt-2014-en.

The DAC's main findings and recommendations

1 Towards a comprehensive Portuguese development effort

Indicator: The member has a broad, strategic approach to development and financing for development beyond aid. This is reflected in overall policies, co-ordination within its government system, and operations

Main findings

Portugal draws on the expertise of its entire public administration to contribute strategically to international development processes and the provision of global public goods.

A strong advocate of the UN 2030 Agenda, Portugal has actively supported the inclusion of Sustainable Development Goal 16, which calls for peaceful and stable societies, as well as Goal 5 on gender equality and woman's rights and Goal 14 on the conservation and sustainable use of oceans and seas.

Portugal has a close relationship with other Portuguese-speaking countries, many of which are its key development partners. It works with them to share information and adopt common positions at the international level on sustainable development issues. As part of its engagement with the Community of Portuguese Speaking Countries (CPLP), for example, it is leading the development of a collective maritime strategy for the sustainable management of the oceans and the seas.

Portugal is committed to ensuring its policies beyond official development assistance (ODA) have a positive impact on partner countries. Since the 2010 peer review, Portugal's Council of Ministers has adopted a legal resolution on policy coherence for development. Seven key policy issues have been identified as critical, and the institutional mechanisms for addressing coherence across ministries have been strengthened.

Building on this progress, Portugal could strengthen analysis and monitoring of how its policies are affecting developing countries. This will enable it to better identify and resolve policy incoherencies and invest in those policies that can support development.

The country ranks highly on the Centre for Global Development's 2014 Commitment to Development Index due to its low greenhouse gas emissions, strong support for research and development, and relatively high levels of financial transparency.

However, tackling policy inconsistencies in sensitive areas can be a challenge. In 2013 the OECD's Working Group on Anti-Bribery expressed some concern over Portugal's lack of progress in prosecuting foreign bribery allegations involving Portuguese companies working abroad due to the difficulties in the gathering of evidence and to obtain answers to mutual legal assistance requests.

Portugal's 2015 follow-up report to the review on Anti-Bribery has shown positive developments. The country is addressing legal loopholes and has initiated a number of new investigations of alleged cases of foreign bribery. Maintaining progress in this area will be critical if Portugal wants to uphold its commitment to governance, rule of law and human rights in developing countries.

Portugal is aware that ODA alone is not sufficient to meet the development finance needs of its partners and has recognised that it should use its ODA in a more catalytic manner.

Its Development Finance Institute – SOFID – uses a wide range of instruments to leverage private finance. However, SOFID's portfolio remains small, and its investments are tied to companies or consortiums that have at least 20% Portuguese capital. There are also limited synergies between SOFID projects and Portugal's development programmes.

Portugal also wants to enhance its support for the private sector in partner countries by adopting a "mutual benefits approach", delivering gains for partner countries as well as Portuguese businesses.

Camões I.P. – Portugal's principal development body – has prudently postponed elaborating a private sector strategy, aware of its limited capacity. Care will be needed to ensure that when a private sector programme is eventually implemented it does not privilege commercial gain to the detriment of development impact, or tie ODA to the purchase of Portuguese goods and services.

Recommendations

1.1 Building on its strong political commitment to policy coherence for development, Portugal should invest more in analysing and monitoring how its policies in key areas are affecting developing countries and take action to address policy inconsistencies.

1.2 When Portugal develops its approach to private sector development, it should ensure this has a positive development impact and respects the DAC recommendations on aid untying.

2 Portugal's vision and policies for development co-operation

Indicator: Clear political directives, policies and strategies shape the member's development co-operation and are in line with international commitments and guidance

Main findings

Portugal's vision for its development co-operation – the Strategic Concept 2014–2020 – is forward-looking and ambitious. The vision seeks to make Portuguese co-operation more responsive to its partner countries' evolving needs and better aligned with the areas where Portugal believes it has comparative advantage.

This new vision expands the overarching purpose of Portugal's co-operation to include sustainable development alongside its traditional focus on eradicating poverty within a context of respect for human rights, democracy and the rule of law. It has also introduced new focus areas – energy and the sea – and placed greater emphasis on the environment and private sector development.

Portugal's policy vision maintains its geographical focus on Portuguese-speaking African countries, and Timor-Leste. However, the vision calls for more strategic partnerships based on shared responsibilities and interests, signalling a change in how Portugal works with some of these countries. These partnerships could help Portugal to manage the transition beyond ODA to more trade and investment-based relationships with some of its partner countries.

Portugal continues to prioritise tackling poverty and has a strong focus on fragile states. This is supported by a national strategy for security and development, endorsed at the highest political level. Portugal is also beginning to develop a more holistic approach to its humanitarian and development programming. To solidify this progress, Portugal could do more to mitigate the risk of crises in all of its partner countries.

Portugal's multilateral ODA is guided by a well-defined distinct policy which complements its bilateral approach. However, it does not yet use a clear set of criteria for assessing the performance or relevance of the multilateral organisations it funds. Establishing these criteria could enable Portugal to allocate its resources better.

In order to take its policy vision forward Portugal will need to address several challenges. Firstly, the new vision is broad in its remit, and many of the new focus areas lack strategies or guidance. There are no strategies, for example, to guide Portugal's work on energy or the private sector in partner countries. Given the declining ODA budget and the capacity constraints within Camões I.P. Portugal would do well to prioritise a few key areas of work and ensure appropriate guidance to support implementation.

Secondly, the vision does not refer to Portugal's substantial bilateral concessional loan portfolio. This portfolio, managed by the Ministry of Finance, focuses predominately on supporting infrastructure development projects. This absence of a specific reference to concessional lending within the vision and the lack of full integration of loans into country programme processes make it hard for staff to exploit synergies between loans and grants.

Thirdly, Portugal still faces a challenge to integrate fully the cross-cutting policy issues of gender equality and environment into its programming. At the crux of the problem is a lack of capacity within Camões I.P. – which has no dedicated budget for addressing cross-cutting issues and limited in-house expertise on these issues.

Recommendations

2.1 Following its Strategic Concept 2014 – 2020, Portugal should establish a realistic medium-term operational plan that identifies a manageable set of priorities for its programme in line with its funding and expertise capacity. It should also develop appropriate guidance for implementing this plan.

2.2 Portugal should fully integrate its bilateral concessional loans portfolio into its strategic planning and country programming processes in order to exploit synergies.

2.3 Camões I.P. should support programme staff throughout Portugal's public administration to integrate gender equality and the environment into all of Portugal's programmes.

3 Allocating Portugal's development assistance

Indicator: The member's international and national commitments drive aid volume and allocations

Main findings

Portugal's capacity to meet its ODA targets has been compromised by its severe economic recession and the subsequent Economic Adjustment Programme.

ODA has fallen in real terms by -14.9% since 2013 (preliminary data). In 2014, Portugal provided US 419 million as ODA, or 0.19% of its gross national income (GNI) according to the OECD's preliminary figures. Projections indicate that it will not meet its target of providing 0.7% of GNI as ODA in 2015.

Since exiting the adjustment programme in 2014, Portugal's economy has shown signs of improvement, though the country is still in post-programme surveillance. Portugal remains committed to meeting its ODA target when its economy begins to recover. However, its heavy reliance on concessional loans to make up the ODA budget in the absence of an increase in grants could jeopardise this commitment.

Portugal has extended EUR 1.6 billion in credit since 2001 and, as of 2015, beneficiary countries had drawn on EUR 958 million (60%) of this in the form of concessional loans, leaving EUR 602 million unspent. If no new lines are opened or the grant element of ODA does not increase, aid levels could plummet far below 0.19% of GNI when these credit lines expire or are completely drawn on by beneficiary countries. To date, half of the credit lines have already expired and the other half will have expired by the end of 2017. The Portuguese government has indicated that it does not anticipate opening new credit lines in the near future.

To address this concern and reverse budget cuts, Portugal's government should set out a pragmatic plan to make sustainable progress towards delivering 0.7% of its GNI as ODA, including an increase in the grant share of Portugal's total ODA.

Portugal will also need to consider carefully how it distributes ODA in the near future if it wants to assist countries most in need and meet its commitment to reverse the trend of declining ODA to least developed countries (LDCs) made at the OECD Development Assistance Committee High Level Meeting in 2014. According to OECD statistics, 29% of Portugal's total ODA was spent on LDCs in 2013, compared to 40% on average between 2010 and 2011. This declining share reflects the changing status of some of Portugal's partners and the increasing amount of concessional loans Portugal has given to countries not classified as least developed.

As part of its commitment to LDCs, Portugal also needs to ensure that it complies with the DAC's recommendation on terms and conditions on lending to LDCs by providing at least a 90% grant element to these countries. In 2013, Portugal's lending did not meet these terms.

Portugal continues to allocate its bilateral ODA according to its strategic priorities. The programme is highly concentrated in sub-Saharan Africa, where five of its six main partner countries are located. In 2013 98% of Portugal's bilateral country-allocable ODA went to its top ten recipient countries. This is far above the DAC average. It also allocates its bilateral programme in line with its thematic priorities, with the largest amount of its sector-allocable aid focused on social sector support, followed by commodity or programme assistance. The latter reflects its concessional loan portfolio.

Portugal could build on its good allocation practices by reducing project-level fragmentation. Despite a commitment to delivering fewer and bigger projects, Portugal still administers a large number of financially small projects in partner countries. All these small projects require co-ordination, taking up precious administration capacity for Portugal and its partners.

Portugal's multilateral ODA represents 35% of its total ODA and is allocated in line with its strategic priorities. Its share of multilateral aid has fallen since the last peer review, reflecting a strategic decision by the Portuguese government, in the face of cuts, to protect its bilateral commitments to partner countries. Despite these cuts, Portugal has managed to maintain strategic relationships with many of its priority organisations by remaining involved on their boards.

Recommendations

3.1 Portugal should establish time-bound, intermediate targets for meeting its international aid volume commitments as its economy recovers. This plan should include a commitment to increase the grant share of its ODA budget.

3.2 Portugal should reverse the decline in its ODA to least developed countries, and maintain its engagement with countries most in need in line with the 2014 High Level Meeting commitments. Portugal should also comply with the 1978 DAC recommendation on terms and conditions on lending to LDCs.

4 Managing Portugal's development co-operation

Indicator: The member's approach to how it organises and manages its development co-operation is fit for purposes

Main findings

Portugal's complex development co-operation system – involving 57 different public entities, each with its own aid budget and implementation ability – is both an asset and a liability for quality programming.

Involving so many actors in the implementation of development co-operation enables Portugal to draw on the rich and diverse expertise offered by its entire public administration. This is clear in Guinea-Bissau, where six line ministries, in addition to the Ministry of Foreign Affairs and Camões I.P., undertook a joint mission in 2014 to resume institutional co-operation with the government. The presence of so many actors enabled Portugal to explore synergies across its various policy communities and to deliver a comprehensive approach to development that went beyond ODA.

However, this complex system can also pose challenges for delivering a coherent and high quality programme. Despite strengthening co-ordination mechanisms at headquarters and giving its development agency - Camões I.P. - greater oversight, Portugal's current business model for managing this system is under pressure.

Camões I.P. was created in 2012 through the merger of Portugal's former development agency (IPAD) and its language and cultural promotion institute (the Camões Institute). The merger, driven by a public sector reform programme, was aimed primarily at achieving efficiencies, but it was also hoped that it would enhance Portugal's development co-operation impact by enabling greater synergies. Despite being directly responsible for only 7.3% of the ODA budget, Camões I.P. is tasked with directing, co-ordinating and overseeing all of Portugal's development co-operation on behalf of the Ministry of Foreign Affairs. It is also responsible for culture and language promotion.

It is too soon to assess the full impact of the merger on Portugal's ability to carry out effective co-operation. However, it is clear that efficiency has increased through joint support and management functions, and shared offices in the field and at headquarters.

It is also evident, though, that Camões I.P., much like its predecessor organisation IPAD, is finding it hard to fulfil its mandate of co-ordinating and overseeing the whole development programme.

Camões I.P.'s co-ordination powers have been strengthened by making its role of providing a prior opinion on line ministries' projects legally-binding. However, this requirement has not been applied to individual projects funded from credit lines extended by the Ministry of Finance, at present accounting for over half of Portugal's bilateral ODA budget.

Limited capacity due to insufficient human resources is one factor hindering Camões I.P.'s effectiveness. The institute has not had the human resource budget to fill all of its agreed staff posts in 2014. As a result, at the time of the review it lacked dedicated staff to work on humanitarian aid, gender and the private sector.

Rigid recruitment procedures also prevent the institute from hiring specialists at headquarters or retaining their skills in the field over the long term.

However, a more fundamental issue is whether the institute has a realistic mandate, given its organisational set up and financial leverage. As a public institute with only a marginal amount of the ODA budget under its direct control there is a serious question whether it will ever have sufficient authority to co-ordinate and oversee the line ministries' development activities.

The division of labour between Camões I.P. and the Ministry of Foreign Affairs could be clearer. For example, at the time of the review the Ministry of Foreign Affairs' Directorate for Foreign Policy was involved in reviewing the Ministry of Finance's ODA concessional loans, but at no point did the Directorate consult with the institute on these loans to draw on its development expertise and enable the loans to be better integrated into the overall development programme as foreseen in Law 6/2004.

Recommendations

4.1 Portugal should examine its business model to ensure that the entity charged with managing its complex system has a clear and appropriate mandate.

4.2 Portugal should also examine whether this entity has adequate human and financial resources to respond to its mandate.

4.3 Portugal should ensure that its development co-operation is governed by human resources and financial rules and regulations with sufficient flexibility to deliver the programme efficiently.

5 Portugal's development co-operation delivery and partnerships

Indicator: The member's approach to how it delivers its programme leads to quality assistance in partner countries, maximising the impact of its support, as defined by Busan

Main findings

Since the last peer review, Portugal has made progress towards meeting some of its international development effectiveness commitments. Changes to its state budget process have made it easier for it to provide more predictable and long-term funding to partners. Its new Strategic Cooperation Programmes, for example, now all include four to five-year indicative budget commitments.

Partners are involved in the design, monitoring and evaluation of country programmes. This reflects Portugal's firm commitment to country ownership and has resulted in its programmes being highly aligned with partners' priorities, as evidenced in São Tomé and Príncipe. Portugal's joint evaluation process also provides an important mutual accountability mechanism, enabling partners to praise or criticise Portugal's performance.

Its engagement in country-led donor co-ordination practices has increased, in line with the last peer review's recommendations. In Mozambique, for example, it participates actively in the joint donor co-ordination group.

Portugal has also strengthened its work with other development co-operation partners. This includes undertaking more delegated programming, as well as triangular co-operation. For example, it is currently preparing new triangular partnerships with Chile in Mozambique.

In response to the last peer review's recommendations, Portugal is also ensuring its programmes adopt a "do no harm" and "conflict sensitive" approach in fragile states. There is a strong focus on technical military co-operation and rule of law support, reflecting Portugal's whole-of-government approach to development.

However, despite these successes, Portugal is aware that some challenges remain in meeting its commitments to making its aid more effective. Four areas, in particular, warrant attention. Firstly, Portugal is struggling to fulfil its commitment to ensure more of its programming goes through partner country systems. In 2013 only 23% of Portugal's aid to the government sector was delivered through partners' public finance and procurement systems: far below the international aid effectiveness target of 57% by 2015. Portugal does not provide sufficient guidance to help staff to assess partners' systems and adapt their programming to use these systems.

Secondly, Portugal has yet to fully develop strategic relationships with selected CSOs partners. While it has established more multi-year partnerships with its CSOs, it still only funds them on a project-by-project basis and does not have a mechanism for supporting their overall framework of programmes. Framework partnerships could reduce transaction costs and enable Portugal to engage in deeper and more flexible relationships with CSOs.

Thirdly, while Portugal has an effective approach to fragile states, it lacks a single shared context and risk analysis framework to guide all parts of public administration working in fragile states. A shared framework would help Portugal to pool its knowledge and improve its programming.

Fourthly, a very high share of Portugal's ODA is tied to the purchase of Portuguese goods and services: 70% in 2013. This is far above the DAC average (14.3%) and represents a significant increase from the last peer review. This high share goes against Portugal's international aid effectiveness commitments. Studies show that tied aid does not always offer value for money to partner countries. While there is little Portugal can do to reduce the tied aid component of its existing credit lines, given the legal nature of these agreements, it can commit to ensuring it does not enter into further tied aid agreements in other parts of its programming or in future lines of credit.

Recommendations

5.1 Portugal should strengthen its guidance and the incentives for staff to use partner country systems in delivering their programmes.

5.2 Portugal should move towards establishing programme-based framework agreements with selected CSO partners.

5.3 Portugal should establish shared context and risk analysis to guide the numerous public entities actors working in fragile states.

5.4 In future allocations and programmes, Portugal should make every effort to meet the OECD recommendation and its Busan commitments to untying aid.

6 Results management and accountability of Portugal's development co-operation

Indicator: The member plans and manages for results, learning, transparency and accountability.

Main findings

Portugal is putting in place a system that should enable it to better plan and manage for results, improve learning and enhance programme transparency and accountability.

Camões I.P. already requires Portugal's development actors to identify results for each project. Its intention now, as it rolls out its new Strategic Cooperation Programmes with its partner countries, is to ensure that expected results are also identified for each country programme. Timor-Leste's 2014-2017 Strategic Cooperation Programme provides a good example of this, containing a measurable set of objectives for the overall programme and indicators for monitoring progress.

However, at this stage, the expected results identified – both for projects and countries – are limited to outputs and their monitoring is weak. Portugal needs to start identifying and monitoring the outcomes and impacts of its work, too, in order to fully assess the performance of its ODA programme.

Camões I.P has a well-developed evaluation system. Its Evaluation and Audit Division is independent of operations, and has a fixed budget and a rolling three-year evaluation plan. In line with good practice, Camões I.P. includes partner countries in its evaluation cycle. Evaluation findings are discussed by a wide range of stakeholders and Camões I.P. publishes an annual evaluation report, which highlights the progress management has made in implementing evaluation recommendations. This is good practice.

However, there is scope to improve the evaluation practices of the line ministries involved in development co-operation. In particular, there appears to have been no evaluation to date by the Portuguese government of its extensive concessional loan portfolio managed by the Ministry of Finance, which accounts for 41% of Portugal's overall ODA budget. It can also be difficult for Camões I.P. to check whether line ministries implement the recommendations of their own evaluations.

Steps are being taken to improve the evaluation practices of the line ministries. A new evaluation policy currently in draft form would grant Camões I.P.'s Evaluation and Audit Division a clear mandate to evaluate all development co-operation interventions and to assure the quality of evaluations conducted by other line ministries. Camões I.P. is also offering training to improve line ministries' evaluation expertise and it has agreed to evaluate one of Portugal's concessional loan projects.

Portugal's complex development co-operation system requires strong knowledge management mechanisms if lessons are to be shared. No such system is currently in place, which is hampering Portugal from learning from its experiences and improving its practices. The planned establishment of technical working groups under the Inter-Ministerial Commission for Cooperation could be a step in the right direction.

Transparency has improved since the last peer review, with Portugal now publishing forward spending plans and project level data in line with the internationally agreed Common Standard. The development of an integrated information system should further enhance the transparency of Portuguese co-operation.

Camões I.P. has developed its own communication strategy, which aims to increase the visibility of Portuguese development co-operation and build public confidence. Despite this new strategy there is considerable scope for Camões I.P. to tell more stories to external audiences about the impact of Portugal's entire development co-operation system. Camões I.P. produces an annual report online, for example, but at present it only covers its own operations (education and development) and not those of other Portuguese development actors.

Recommendations

6.1 Portugal should ensure that all its country programmes have a clear set of expected outcome-orientated results and that staff regularly monitor progress towards achieving them.

6.2 In order to achieve a more cohesive and co-ordinated programme, Portugal's development actors should share lessons on approaches and results with each other on a regularly basis.

6.3 Portugal should adopt and put into practice the new evaluation policy as soon as possible.

7 Portugal's humanitarian assistance

Indicator: The member contributes to minimising the impact of shocks and crises, and saves lives, alleviates suffering and maintains dignity in crisis and disaster settings

Main findings

Most of Portugal's humanitarian programme is implemented as bilateral responses through the civil protection service, often co-funded by the European Union. Bilateral response operations – mostly in-kind aid – are ably co-ordinated by the Ministry of Interior, building on its domestic co-ordination role. There are good relationships with partner country governments who request relief goods in times of crisis. Civil protection seeks to learn from its international deployments so as to improve future work, which is good practice. Portugal now needs to look for a mechanism to better link its bilateral humanitarian responses to its development co-ordination programmes and the wider humanitarian international response system.

Despite a lack of funds for other humanitarian partners, Portugal continues to support where it can. One example is its support to UNHCR's confidence-building programme for refugees from Western Sahara. Portugal also makes regular contributions to the Central Emergency Response Fund's global pooled funding mechanism.

To ensure that the humanitarian programme is fit for the future, Portugal will need to work on some key areas. In August 2015 Portugal issued a new operational strategy for its humanitarian programme; this is a good start and could be used as a basis to address the following issues:

- The lack of a clear and shared understanding of how to build on Portugal's comparative advantage to deliver effective humanitarian action.
- Ad hoc, political decisions over where, and how, to respond to crises. This creates the risk of misperceptions about Portugal's respect for humanitarian principles such as independence and impartiality - although Portugal is careful to align its bilateral responses to requests from partner countries.
- Unpredictable and last-minute funding to most humanitarian partners, stemming from the ad hoc approach to the humanitarian programme.
- Uncertainty over how to leverage Portugal's domestic crisis preparedness skills to systematically build the capacity of civil protection services in partner countries.

The operational strategy may also allow Portugal to advocate for a dedicated humanitarian budget line and thus increase its overall humanitarian aid, in line with international burden-sharing agreements.

Better communication of the results of Portugal's humanitarian assistance could help build political consensus around the need for a bigger and broader humanitarian programme.

Finally, Portugal lacks a civil-military policy and standard procedures. This is a risk given the regular use of military and civil defence assets to deliver relief goods and provide technical support in humanitarian responses. Portugal will need clear guidance on their use if it is to demonstrate that it has complied with international agreements.

Recommendations

7.1 Portugal should build on its new operational strategy for the humanitarian programme to ensure that future responses are predictable, leverage Portugal's comparative advantage, and are in line with humanitarian principles.

7.2 Portugal should set out guidelines for the use of military and civil defence assets in its humanitarian response, in line with international agreements.

Secretariat's report

Chapter 1: Towards a comprehensive Portuguese development effort

Global development issues

Portugal takes a strategic approach to addressing global public risks, drawing on expertise from across government to contribute to a range of international processes and policy debates. Within international fora, it works actively with Portuguese speaking countries, many of which are its key development partners, to share information and, where possible, adopt common positions on sustainable development issues.

Portugal contributes to supporting global public goods

Portugal draws on the expertise of its entire government to influence global development debates on gender equality; security and development; climate change; and the oceans and seas. Portugal is:

- actively engaged in the United Nations post-2015 negotiations and has developed a national position paper outlining its priorities and positions (Camões I.P., 2015). It has been a strong supporter of the UN's Sustainable Development Goal 16, which calls for peaceful and stable societies, Goal 5 on gender equality, and Goal 14 on the sustainable conservation and use of oceans and seas;
- using its election to the UN Human Rights Council in October 2014 to focus attention on tackling violence against women and protecting the most vulnerable groups and people, among other issues;
- working with the Community of Portuguese Speaking Countries (CPLP)[1] to develop a collective maritime strategy aimed at encouraging the sustainable management of oceans and seas.

Its engagement with other Portuguese speaking countries at the international level, many of which are its development co-operation partners, has enabled Portugal to share information and, where possible, adopt common positions on key development issues. Its strategic participation with the Community of Portuguese Speaking Countries on climate change issues, for example, has resulted in a network of Portuguese speaking countries being created to meet alongside the Conference of State Parties to the UN Framework Convention on Climate Change. The network exchanges information about negotiating groups and, given CPLP membership, allows the group to have insider knowledge on positions held by the G-77, EU, G20, and the least developed countries and small islands developing states groupings.

Policy coherence for development

Indicator: Domestic policies support or do not harm developing countries

Portugal has a strong political commitment to tackling policy coherence for development and there is a high level of awareness of the issue across its public administration. However, it needs to make further progress with implementation, identifying and resolving incoherencies between its domestic and development policies.

Solid political commitment to policy coherence for development

Portugal's commitment to policy coherence for development has been strengthened by its Council of Ministers adopting a legal resolution on the issue in 2010 (GOP, 2010). Portugal's domestic framework follows EU standards (Council of the EU, 2009) and its development strategy – the Strategic Concept 2014-2020 (GOP, 2014) – sets policy coherence for development as one of the main operating principles guiding development co-operation.[2] Seven policy areas are considered particularly relevant for seeking coherence: trade, finance, climate change, the oceans and seas, food security, migration and security.

Portugal's inter-ministerial commission has a mandate to address policy coherence for development

In response to last peer review's recommendations (OECD, 2011a), Portugal's Inter-Ministerial Commission for Co-operation mandate has been broadened to include addressing policy coherence for development as well as co-ordinating the development programme (GOP, 2013). The Commission has also started to meet at the highest political level[3] strengthening its leverage across government.

To enhance capacity, a focal point has been identified inside each line ministry. These focal points are tasked with determining which policies in their respective areas are incoherent with development and putting forward proposals to the Commission for how to promote greater coherence. Portugal is also keen to establish sectorial inter-ministerial groups to address specific coherence issues as and when they are needed (Camões I.P., 2015). This should be pursued to enable relevant ministries to analyse incoherence in a cross-sectorial manner.

In fulfilling its new dual mandate the Commission should be conscious that improving co-ordination and dealing with policy incoherence are two different things – the two principles currently appear conflated in the government's Strategic Concept. While they are related, there are instances of incoherent policies which cannot be solved simply by improving co-ordination.

Good awareness across government of policy coherence

There is a high level of understanding across the Portuguese government of the importance of policy coherence for development, as revealed in peer review interviews with several government agencies in Lisbon. To date, however (as of June 2015), there has been limited analysis to identify potential incoherencies within these policy areas and there is no clear time frame for carrying out this analysis. Camões I.P., Portugal's development institute, is now working to encourage further analysis of domestic policies. For that purpose, it is training all line ministries' focal points as well as NGOs implementing projects funded by Portuguese aid. An awareness-raising event for members of parliament also took place in 2015.

Scope to strengthen monitoring

Monitoring progress towards policy coherence for development is still a challenge, as noted in the last peer review (OECD, 2010). In order to learn from peers, Camões I.P. has commissioned a study in partnership with the Swiss Agency for Development Cooperation to identify policy coherence indicators used by other European Union (EU) countries (ECDPM, 2015). This is expected to inform the development of Portugal's monitoring system. Portugal does have an interesting experience with supporting partner countries' monitoring efforts, as evidenced in Cabo Verde (Box 1.1), but this experience has not yet led to any reforms of Portugal's domestic policies.

Portugal made a special effort to promote the topic of policy coherence during its EU presidency in 2007 and contributes to the EU biennial report on policy coherence for development in accordance with its national laws. It does not report on a regular basis, though, to its national parliament on progress in this area. Establishing a regular discussion in parliament on this issue would enhance national debate and accountability.

Box 1.1 Increasing policy coherence awareness in Cabo Verde

Portugal and the EU have co-financed an innovative three-year project in Cabo Verde to build the capacity of civil society and parliamentarians to monitor policy incoherence in the domestic policies of the Cabo Verde government. Although policy coherence for development has been mainly used in the context of donors ensuring their own domestic policies do not threaten development objectives, the concept can also be applied at the partner country level (OECD, 2012).

The project focuses on three policy areas (fisheries, agriculture and environment) and seeks to understand, through research and analysis, what factors within these areas are contributing to poor development results and how this might be rectified by greater policy coherence. In the agriculture area, for example, problems with transport (i.e. maintenance of paved roads) were identified as contributing to limited agricultural development in the settlement of Achada Mitra (IMVF, 2014).

The project has successfully involved 54 members of the National and Municipal Assemblies (the National Assembly is composed of 75 members). A website, managed by an NGO platform, has been set up to function as a repository of information and receive indication of potential policy incoherencies (www.coerenciascv.org).

Source: Interview conducted on 8 June 2015; OECD (2012); IMVF (2014); Assembleia Nacional de Cabo Verde (n.d).

Progress in tackling policy inconsistencies is slow

Portugal was ranked fifth out of 27 countries on the 2014 Commitment to Development Index[4] – an independent initiative that monitors the degree to which countries have development-friendly policies. Its high score is due to its low greenhouse gas emissions,[5] its strong support for research and development linked to the dissemination of technology in developing countries, and its relatively high levels of financial transparency.

Despite this success, the political will to address policy inconsistencies in sensitive areas can be a challenge. One case in point is the OECD Working Group on Bribery's 2013 review, which highlighted concern over the limited progress Portugal had made in prosecuting bribery allegations involving Portuguese companies abroad due to difficulties in mutual legal assistance requests (OECD, 2013).[6]

It is positive to note that since this review Portugal has started to take action to address this concern. The follow up report presented by Portugal to the working group in 2015 highlights that four new investigative procedures have been initiated and that legal loopholes are being addressed. Given that Africa is the country's second most important trading partner and a significant number of Portuguese companies operate in the region, failure to pursue bribery would be inconsistent with Portugal's principle of contributing to governance and rule of law.

In addition, Camões I.P. has successfully followed up on the last OECD DAC peer review recommendation to improve corruption risk management and is establishing a whistleblowing mechanism for staff (Chapter 5). Camões I.P., for example, now cross-checks companies with which it conducts business against debarment lists published by multilateral development agencies. This is to avoid doing business with those that have been convicted of corruption. The Ministry of Justice, in turn, is partnering with the United Nations Office on Drugs and Crime (UNODC) to provide training on investigation and prosecution for judges and magistrates in partner countries.

Financing for development

Indicator: The member engages in development finance in addition to ODA

Portugal wants to use its official development assistance (ODA) in a more catalytic manner and has signalled a desire to increase its support for private sector development in partner countries through a mutual benefits approach. While its capacity in this area is currently limited, Portugal does have a small development finance institution – SOFID – that deploys a variety of instruments for leveraging finance. SOFID's funds, however, are tied to Portuguese companies and there are limited synergies between its projects and other ODA-funded projects at present. Portugal tracks the totality of its resource flows for development and makes this information available to all key stakeholders.

Portugal has prudently postponed developing a private sector strategy due to capacity constraints

Portugal's development co-operation strategy – the Strategic Concept 2014-2020 – recognises the importance of development finance as a complement to ODA and signals a desire to assist with private sector development in partner countries "by supporting a favourable business environment and by creating partnerships" (GOP, 2014). Portugal's approach is one of mutual benefit: allowing partner countries to benefit from resources, knowledge and technology sharing, while also giving Portuguese companies greater access to foreign markets. Mutual benefit is not problematic so long as Portugal ensures that it does not privilege commercial gain at the detriment of development impact. It should also not result in Portugal tying more of its aid[7] to the goods and services of Portuguese companies, given that this may not always represent value for money for Portugal's development partners.[8]

At present Portugal's capacity to take this agenda forward is limited. There is no private sector strategy in place to guide its work, and Camões I.P. has no staff with private sector expertise. Camões I.P. has prudently postponed drafting a strategy until it can acquire greater know-how (Chapter 4 and 5). It expects to learn from current debates on total official support to sustainable development, the sustainable development goals (SDGs) and financing for development, as well as its engagement in relevant fora in which private sector engagement is discussed. Its initiative in Mozambique may also provide useful lessons for private sector engagement (Box 1.2).

Box 1.2. Using ODA to foster indigenous private sector development in Mozambique

The Business Fund for Portuguese Cooperation in Mozambique is a joint initiative between Camões I.P., the Mozambican Institute for the Promotion of Small and Middle Enterprises, and the Mozambican Bank Association. Established in 2014, the USD 13 million fund supports Mozambican small and medium-sized enterprises by covering the risks involved for banks wishing to finance them. Five proposals submitted by small business owners have already been received and are being assessed. It is too early to measure the degree to which this support is developing the indigenous private sector, but it offers an important experience for Camões I.P.

Source: Interview conducted on 18 June 2015; Camões I.P., IPEME and AMB (n.d.).

Development finance instruments exist but are tied to Portuguese companies

The *Sociedade para o Financiamento do Desenvolvimento* (SOFID) is Portugal's main instrument for leveraging private flows for development. In place since 2007, this public/private agency is housed within the Ministry of Finance. It has a wide range of financial instruments at its disposal – including long-term loans, guarantees and mezzanine finance and equity investments.

However, SOFID's portfolio remains small (USD 17.58 million in 2015) and its investments are tied to those companies or consortiums that have at least 20% Portuguese capital. Synergies between SOFID's projects and those implemented by Camões I.P. or other line ministries are also limited. In most cases, SOFID's projects are in areas where Portugal's other development actors are not active and in countries outside Camões I.P.'s six priority countries.[9]

The last peer review recommended that Portugal's former development agency sit on the governing board of SOFID to ensure greater engagement (OECD, 2010; and see Annex A). While Camões I.P. participates in SOFID's Strategy Committee – a consultative body – it does not participate on the board. The last review also called for an evaluation of SOFID's development impact to assess its performance. A review of SOFID's activities has been agreed and will be conducted by an external body during 2015-16. This evaluation is an opportunity for both agencies, as well as their respective parent ministries (Ministry of Finance and Ministry of Foreign Affairs), to reflect on how to foster synergies among the private and development co-operation sectors.

Large private flows to developing countries

Since 2013, Camões I.P. has been tracking and reporting to the OECD-DAC on non-ODA financial flows to developing countries. In 2013, private flows from Portugal to developing countries were more than three times greater than ODA flows, representing USD 1 776 million. The level of remittances from Portugal to developing countries stood at USD 317 million in 2013.

Notes

1. The Community of Portuguese-Speaking Countries (CPLP) is an inter-governmental organisation which seeks to provide a forum for greater political co-operation among (Portuguese-speaking) nations. It was established in 1996.

2. The principles are coherence/co-ordination (to reinforce co-ordination, monitoring and dialogue between partners, as well as complementarity of actions), concentration (to foster larger programmes within geographical and sectorial priorities), ownership (to improve sustainability, based on capacity development) and partnership (to share capacities and resources, through diversification of partnerships).

3. The official statutes of the Commission indicate the following as members: Ministries of Finance, National Defence, Internal Administration, Justice, Parliamentary Affairs, Economy and Employment, Agriculture, Sea, Environment and Territorial Arrangements, Health, Education and Science, Solidarity and Social Security, the State Secretary of the Presidency of the Council of Ministries, the Deputy State Secretary of the Prime Ministry, and the State Secretary for Culture (GOP, 2013). Other institutions are also represented on the Commission.

4. The Commitment to the Development Index produced by the Center for Global Development analyses policy areas in developed countries that have an impact on developing countries. Twenty seven countries were ranked in the 2014 Index. Portugal ranked 12th for its aid policies, 17th for trade, 8th for finance, 22nd for migration, 5th for environment, 9th for security and 3rd for technology.

5. Portugal is a champion of renewable energy use among OECD countries. In 2009, renewable energy accounted for 21% of primary energy supply and 38% of electricity production. This is far above the OECD Europe average. (OECD, 2011).

6. The OECD Working Group on Bribery reviews members' implementation of the OECD Convention on Combating Bribery of Foreign Public Officials in International Business Transactions.

7. Portugal's share of ODA that is tied is already high, accounting for 70% of bilateral ODA in 2013 (Chapter 5).

8. Evidence cited by the OECD shows that tied aid "can increase the costs of a development project by as much as 15 to 30 percent." (OECD, n.d.).

9. SOFID works in the telecommunication, trade and services, agribusiness and manufacturing sectors. It is present in Mexico, Morocco, Brazil, South Africa, Mozambique and Angola.

Bibliography

Government sources

Agência Portuguesa Do Meio Ambiente (n.d.), Fundos Ambientais, www.apambiente.pt/index.php?ref=17&subref=162 (accessed 8 June 2015).

Camões I.P. (2014), *Documento de Posição de Portugal sobre a Agenda pós 2015*, Camões, I.P. (Camões Instituto da Cooperação e da Lingua Portugal), Lisbon.

Camões I.P., IPEME and AMB (n.d.): "Fundo empresarial da Cooperacão Portugesa".

GOP (2014), *Conceito Estratégico da Cooperação Portuguesa 2014-2020,* [Strategic Concept for Portuguese Development Cooperation 2014-2020], GOP (Government of Portugal), Lisbon. http://d3f5055r2rwsy1.cloudfront.net/images/cooperacao/conctestratg1420.pdf.

GOP (2013), "Portaria 173/2013, de 7 de Maio", *Diário da República,* No. 87, 7 May 2013, GOP, Lisbon, http://dre.tretas.org/dre/308974/.

GOP (2010), "Resolução do Conselho de Ministros No. 82/2010", *Diário da República,* No. 214, GOP, Lisbon, www.coerencia.pt/_files/ResolucaodoConselhodeMinistros82-2010.pdf.

GOP (2006), "Decreto lei No 71/2006", *Diário da Républica,* No. 60, GOP, Lisbon, https://poseur.portugal2020.pt/media/3989/decreto-lei-que-cria-o-fundo-portugu%C3%AAs-de-carbono.pdf.

Other sources

Assembleia Nacional de Cabo Verde (n.d.), Deputados da VIII Legislatura, www.parlamento.cv/deputados2.aspx (accessed 1 August 2015).

CGD (2014), *Commitment to Development Index 2014*, CGD (Center for Global Development), Washington, DC, www.cgdev.org/publication/ft/commitment-development-index-2014?callout=1-4.

Council of the European Union (2009), "Council conclusions on Policy Coherence for Development (PCD)", 2974th External Relations Council meeting, Brussels, 17 November 2009, www.consilium.europa.eu/uedocs/cms_data/docs/pressdata/en/gena/111278.pdf.

ECDPM (2015), "Use of PCD indicators by a selection of EU member States: A brief analysis and overview", *Discussion Paper,* No. 171, ECDPM (European Centre for Development Policy Management), http://ecdpm.org/publications/policy-coherence-indicators-eu/.

EU (2013), *EU 2013 Report on Policy Coherence for Development*, EU (European Union), Brussels, https://ec.europa.eu/europeaid/node/45425.

IMVF (2014), *Um Estudo de Caso no Sector Agrícola: Coerência das Políticas para o Desenvolvimento, Desafio para uma Cidadania Activa em Cabo Verde*, IMVF (Instituto Marquês de Valle Flôr), http://issuu.com/imvf/docs/estudo_de_caso_agricultura_final.

OECD (2013), *Phase 3 Report on Implementing the OECD Anti-Bribery Convention in Portugal*, OECD Publishing, Paris, www.oecd.org/daf/anti-bribery/Portugalphase3reportEN.pdf.

OECD (2011), *OECD Environmental Performance Reviews: Portugal 2011*, OECD Publishing, Paris, http://dx.doi.org/10.1787/9789264097896-en.

OECD (2010), *OECD Development Assistance Peer Reviews: Portugal 2010*, OECD Publishing, Paris, http://dx.doi.org/10.1787/9789264098312-en.

OECD (n.d.), "Untied aid", www.oecd.org/dac/untied-aid/ (accessed 1 July 2015).

Chapter 2: Portugal's vision and policies for development co-operation

Policies, strategies and commitments

Indicator: A clear policy vision and solid strategies guide the programme

Portugal has a long-term vision for its development programme that is owned across the whole of government. The vision recognises the evolving needs of partner countries and calls for more strategic partnerships in order to manage relationships as they transition beyond ODA. However, the vision is ambitious with many of the new focus areas not supported by strategies or guidance. Given the current capacity constraints within Camões I.P., Portugal could benefit from prioritising a few key areas for implementation and ensuring that these areas are supported by appropriate guidance.

Portugal's forward-looking vision calls for strategic partnerships to help with transitions

Portugal's Strategic Concept (2014 -2020) provides an ambitious vision for its development assistance (GOP, 2014). The strategy, developed through a consultative process as recommended in the last peer review, is owned by the entire government.[1] The international principles for effective development co-operation, as confirmed in Busan are also embedded in the strategy (HL4, 2011).

The Strategic Concept represents continuity, rather than a rupture, with Portugal's previous development co-operation strategy (MNE/IPAD, 2006). The over-arching purpose of co-operation remains the eradication of poverty within a context of respect for human rights, democracy and the rule of law. However, it does include a new complementary goal of achieving sustainable development in partner countries. New sectors have also been identified, such as energy and the sea, and there is a stronger emphasis on the environment and private sector development. These new focus areas respond to the changing development landscape and partner countries' evolving needs (Davies and Pickering, 2015). They are also where Portugal believes it has a comparative advantage.

In light of the rising incomes and growing geopolitical relevance of some of Portugal's partner countries, the Strategic Concept signals a desire by Portugal to move towards more strategic partnerships based on "donor-partner shared responsibilities, with mutual benefits" (GOP, 2014). These partnerships could help Portugal to manage the transition beyond ODA to relationships based more on trade and investment.

Aware that this policy was developed prior to the conclusions of the UN's post-2015 discussions, Portugal has commissioned research to look at how it can better position its development co-operation in light of the outcomes of these discussions. The research, carried out by the European Centre for Development Policy Management, will be used to refine its strategic vision in the coming years.[2]

Portugal's ambitious vision requires prioritisation given capacity constraints in Camões I.P.

While the Strategic Concept is undoubtedly forward-looking, it is broad in its remit. Given Portugal's declining ODA budget and the capacity constraints within Camões I.P. (Chapters 3 and 4) Portugal will need to prioritise a few key areas for implementation, matching its ambition to its present resources. The policy is also not yet supported by guidance, which makes it difficult to implement on the ground. There is no guidance, for example, to support Portugal's work on energy or private sector in partner countries or until very recently its humanitarian efforts (Chapter 7).

Approach to allocating bilateral and multilateral aid

Indicator: The rationale for allocating aid and other resources is clear and evidence-based

Portugal has separate rationales for allocating its bilateral grants and concessional loans, reflecting the two instruments' different attributes. Bilateral grants are guided by a strong geographical focus, but the rationale for sector allocations within country is less clear. Concessional loans are focused predominately on infrastructure, but are not fully integrated into Portugal's policy vision or country programming. As a result Portugal is missing opportunities to exploit synergies between its loans and grant portfolios. While Portugal has a well-defined multilateral strategy for guiding its allocations, it lacks a clear set of criteria for assessing the performance and relevance of the multilateral organisations it funds.

Grant ODA has a clear geographic focus and sector concentration is improving

Portugal's bilateral grants continue to be governed by a clear geographic focus which centres on Portuguese-speaking African countries (known as the PALOP) (Mozambique, Angola, Guinea Bissau, Sao Tome and Principe, and Cabo Verde), and Timor-Leste. The majority of these partner countries are classified as least developed countries (LDCs), and two are considered to be fragile states.[3]

Portugal's rationale for allocating grant funding to its partner countries is complex given the country's fragmented institutional set up for development co-operation (Chapter 4). The need to accommodate the demands of Portugal's numerous line ministries – each with their own ODA budget (Table 3.1, Chapter 3) and sector expertise – alongside partner countries' needs and Portugal's broader national interest, can pose problems for delivering a strategic and focused programme within countries. In recognition of this challenge, and in line with the last peer review's recommendation, Portugal has identified greater concentration as one of four operating principles (GOP, 2014). To put this principle into practice it has established a clear target of supporting only three or four sectors in each partner country, in line with its EU commitments (GOP, 2014). Portugal is also keen to deliver larger programmes in order to achieve economies of scale, reduce transaction costs and enhance development impact. As Portugal negotiates its Strategic Cooperation Programmes with partner countries, efforts should be made to ensure line ministries join up their efforts to deliver bigger and fewer projects (Chapter 3).

Credit lines support infrastructure but are not fully integrated into Portugal's vision

Over half of Portugal's bilateral ODA in 2013 was allocated as concessional loans delivered via credit lines managed by the Ministry of Finance (Chapter 3). Portugal mainly deploys these credit lines to finance infrastructure projects in developing countries, in recognition of partners' substantial financing needs in this area (and the business opportunities these loans provide for Portuguese companies). The rationale for determining which countries receive credit lines and how much they should get, though, is less clear.[4]

This instrument firmly puts partner country governments in the driving seat, enabling them to draw on concessional loans, as and when they want, and to propose projects. However, credit lines remain heavily tied to the purchase of Portuguese goods and services (Chapter 5). The instrument is also not fully integrated into Portugal's development policy vision[5] or country programming processes (Chapter 4). Infrastructure development is not mentioned as a priority in Portugal's Strategic Concept, and there is no policy guidance to assist with project approvals, monitoring or evaluation. The lack of an integrated approach means that Portugal is missing opportunities to exploit synergies among its loans and grant portfolios in partner countries. For example, Portugal might have been able to promote greater support for renewable energy infrastructure projects to complement its environmental grant projects. To date, only 7% of Portugal's credit lines have been spent on renewable energy infrastructure (Camões I.P., 2015).

Sound multilateral strategy , but Portugal lacks clear criteria for assessing the performance of multilateral organisations

Portugal's multilateral strategy is well-focused and provides a sound rationale for allocating aid across different multilateral organisations (MNA/IPAD, 2009). Synergies between its multilateral and bilateral grant assistance are exploited in the field, and Portugal co-finances multilateral organisations' projects in its partner countries to a limited extent (Chapter 3).[6]

Camões I.P. regularly assesses the development performance of the multilateral organisations it funds. It does this by drawing on the organisations own evaluation reports and consulting with staff working in Portugal's delegations and missions to multilateral organisations and embassies in key partner countries. These assessments are taken into consideration by the ministries responsible for allocating the bulk of Portugal's multilateral aid – the ministries of foreign affairs and finance. However, Camões I.P. does not yet have a clear set of criteria for measuring multilateral organisations' performance and relevance. Establishing a set of criteria would enable Portugal to more easily compare performance across organisations. Sharing these criteria and the assessments with the multilateral organisations would also enhance accountability and learning.

Portugal works actively to help multilateral organisations improve their effectiveness, as demonstrated by its support for enhancing the organisational performance of the Community of Portuguese Speaking Countries (CPLP).

Policy focus

Indicator: Fighting poverty, especially in LDCs and fragile states, is prioritised

Portugal has a clear policy vision for eradicating poverty, but project and programme design could be informed by more rigorous poverty analyses. Despite a pragmatic and flexible approach to working in fragile states, further work is required to ensure a truly holistic approach to its humanitarian and development programming. Camões I.P. is also trying to fulfil its objective of integrating gender equality and the environment across Portugal's entire co-operation programme, but capacity is a constraint.

There is scope to enhance poverty analysis at the project level; ODA guided by a clear strategic focus on fragility

Portugal's policy vision and sector strategies focus on interventions that reduce poverty and assist vulnerable groups such as girls, woman and children. There is also evidence of poverty-focused programmes in the field, such as Portugal's work on promoting social protection systems in partner countries. Nonetheless, poverty guidance at the project level could be enhanced. The standardised project proposal template and project eligibility criteria used by most line ministries are not sufficiently rigorous and robust poverty analyses are not yet informing all project or programme design.

Although fragility is not a formal selection criterion for partner countries, two of Portugal's partners are considered fragile states: Timor-Leste and Guinea-Bissau. These countries, along with São Tome and Principe are also members of the G7+ group - countries which are or have been affected by conflict. Fragility also has a prominent role in the new Strategic Concept (GOP, 2014). In line with this, Portugal seeks to influence the global development agenda, drawing on its experience in peace, security and development.

Portugal could do more to help its partner countries to mitigate risks

There are some ad hoc examples of holistic action involving the humanitarian and development programmes. This includes the Ministry of Health's work to support medical laboratories in Guinea-Bissau in the face of a looming Ebola crisis. However, Portugal could do more to mitigate the risk of crises in developing countries, thereby protecting its development investments and overall progress towards sustainable development objectives. Leveraging the skills of Portugal's civil protection service to build response capacity in partner countries could be a useful start (Chapter 7).

Engagement in fragile situations is guided by a national security and development strategy

Portugal has a pragmatic, flexible approach to working in fragile states. The national strategy on security and development has been endorsed at the highest political level (GOP, 2009). This is complemented by individual ministry policies which follow the approach taken by the national strategy. International policy approaches to tackling fragile states have changed considerably since 2009, however; Portugal's policies will need to be updated to reflect these.[7] Portugal plans to do update its policies in 2016.

Weak capacity is hindering progress on cross-cutting issues

Portugal's strong domestic political commitment to the environment and gender equality has yet to be fully mirrored within its development co-operation programmes.[8] Camões I.P. has made some progress since the last peer review to integrate the environment into its programming. However, monitoring is not comprehensive.[9] The crux of the problem is a lack of capacity within Camões I.P, which has no dedicated gender focal point, for example, to champion, support and monitor this issue and no specific budget for cross-cutting activities (OECD, 2014). Portugal's new Strategic Concept does not include a plan for how to improve management of cross-cutting issues, despite this being recommended in the last peer review (OECD, 2011a). Indeed, if anything, the Strategic Concept has confused stakeholders as to which issues Portugal considers as cross-cutting in its development co-operation. Portugal's Strategic Concept identifies only two cross-cutting issues – gender equality and children's rights – the latter is a new cross-cutting issue for Portugal. The environment is treated as a sector priority area in the Strategic Concept and not a cross cutting issue. However, the peer review team was informed in interviews in Lisbon that the environment would remain a cross-cutting issue.

The environment and climate change are beginning to be integrated into programming

Portugal's share of ODA dedicated to the environment has increased since the last peer review. On average 8% of its bilateral ODA between 2011 and 2013 were allocated to the environment. The DAC average over this period was 23%. The majority of Portugal's environment focused ODA was allocated for climate change mitigation, especially renewable energy.

A number of factors have contributed to Portugal's increasing share of environment-related ODA:

- the establishment of Portugal's Carbon Fund[10] as part of its Fast Start[11] commitments, which has provided new sources of financing for climate-related development projects
- the release of guidelines requiring that all grant project proposals consider environmental issues, which has raised awareness of the need to factor in the environment at the design stage of projects[12]
- a new focal point within Camões I.P., which has strengthened staff support
- the creation of a joint working group involving Camões I.P. and the Ministry of Environment, Spatial Planning and Regional Development[13] to assess the environmental impact of all Camões I.P.'s project proposals, which has brought greater rigour to programme design.

The joint working group, in particular, provides a good model for enabling Camões I.P. to draw on expertise across the Portuguese government. This group is currently confined to scrutinising Camões I.P. projects, which represent only a marginal amount of Portugal's overall ODA (7.3%). Consideration should be given to expanding its mandate so that it assesses Portugal's substantial ODA infrastructure loan portfolio administered by the Ministry of Finance. The peer review team was informed that the Ministry of Finance holds regular discussions with the Ministry of Environment in order to get their views on the environmental impact of proposed loan projects; the Ministry of Finance also abides by the OECD's guidelines on Export Credits, in particular the common approach to social and environmental due diligence (OECD, 2012).[14]However, Camões I.P. is not consulted by the Ministry of Finance on loan proposals, nor does it regularly receive information from the Ministry on how the monitoring or evaluation of cross-cutting issues within loan projects is progressing.

ODA for gender equality is decreasing

In 2013, 30% of Portugal's bilateral sector allocable aid had gender equality and women's empowerment as a principal or significant objective. This compares favourably with the DAC average of 33%. However, Portugal's ODA for gender equality has decreased as a share of ODA since 2012 when it stood at 38%. Portugal does have policy guidance on gender equality (IPAD,2010) which includes indicators for measuring progress on gender equality in areas like health, education and security and defence. However, the lack of in-house expertise within Camões I.P. to support staff is hindering it from making further progress.

Notes

1. The Strategic Concept was adopted by Portugal's Council of Ministers in February 2014.

2. The research will look at how Portuguese development co-operation should adapt and respond to the rise of emerging new donors and new sources of development finance, among other things.

3. Mozambique, Guinea-Bissau, Sap Tome and Príncipe, Angola and Timor-Leste are all considered least developed countries according to the UN in 2015. East Timor and Guinea-Bissau are considered fragile states in 2015 according to the OECD's unofficial list of fragile states (OECD, n.d. a).

4. While many partner countries have been given credit lines (Cabo Verde, Angola, Mozambique and Sao Tome and Príncipe), other non-partner countries have also been given access to credit lines (Morocco and China).

5. The Strategic Concept makes no reference to the credit lines or infrastructure development.

6. For example, in Guinea-Bissau Portugal is supporting a UNICEF education project and a UNFPA sexual and reproductive health project.

7. More on changes in the international policy environment for fragility can be found in the OECD's (n.d. b), "International engagement in fragile states", www.oecd.org/dac/governance-peace/conflictandfragility/iefs.htm.

8. Portugal has a National Strategy for Sustainable Development (GOP, 2015) and a National Plan for Equality, Citizenship and Gender (CIG, 2014). It has also established a Commission for Citizenship and Gender Equality and a Counsellor for Equality to promote implementation of the National Plan.

9. The peer review team was informed during the mission to Lisbon that not all projects were monitored to assess progress against gender equality or the environment and climate change.

10. The Portuguese Carbon Fund (PCF) is a domestic fund established in 2006 with the main objective of supporting actions at the national level to meet the Portuguese commitments under Kyoto Protocol. After 2009 a window was opened in the fund in order to also support climate change activities in developing countries. This fund is part of Portugal's Fast Start Finance commitments (see next note) and is an innovative instrument for purchasing emissions credits on the international market.

11. During the 15th Conference of the Parties to the United Nations Framework Convention on Climate Change developed countries pledged to provide new and additional resources, approaching USD 30 billion for the period 2010-12, to help developing countries respond to climate change. Allocation is to be balanced between mitigation and adaptation. This collective commitment has come to be known as "fast-start finance".

12. These guidelines (Camões I.P., n.d. a) also request that programme managers demonstrate how gender equality is being addressed in project design.

13. The working group was originally set up to approve Fast Start projects only, but has since been expanded to include all Camões I.P. projects.

14 Portugal is helping its partners to build their capacity to undertake environmental impact assessments through its support of the Network of Environmental Assessment Associations. This network includes organisations working in Brazil, Angola, Mozambique, Cabo Verde and Guinea-Bissau.

Bibliography

Government sources

Camões I.P. (2015), *Memorandum of Portugal*, 16 March 2015, Camões I.P. (Camões Instituto da Cooperação e da Lingua Portugal), Lisbon.

Camões I.P. (n.d. a), *Apresentação de Propostas de Programas, Projetos ou Ações de Cooperação para o Desenvolvimento: Instruções de Preenchimento* [Program Proposals, Projects and Cooperative Action for Development: Form Instructions], Camões I.P., Lisbon, http://d3f5055r2rwsy1.cloudfront.net/images/cooperacao/formulario_apres_ppa_instrucoes.pdf.

Camões I.P. (n.d. b) *Procedimentos para Elegibilidade e Análise de Programas, Projetos e Ações de Cooperação* [Procedures for Eligibility and Analysis of Programmes, Projects and Co-operation Activities], Camões I.P., Lisbon, http://d3f5055r2rwsy1.cloudfront.net/images/cooperacao/elegibilidade_analise_ppa.pdf.

CCGE (Commission for Citizenship and Gender Equality) (2014) V National Plan for gender equality, citizenship and non-discrimination (2014-2017), Commission for Citizenship and Gender Equality, Lisbon.

GOP (2015), *Estratégia Nacional de Desenvolvimento Sustentável. ENDS 2015* [National Sustainable Development Strategy ENDS 2015], GOP (Government of Portugal), Lisbon. www.apambiente.pt/index.php?ref=16&subref=143&sub2ref=734.

GOP (2014), *Conceito Estratégico da Cooperação Portuguesa 2014-2020,* (Strategic Concept for Portuguese Development Cooperation 2014-2020*)*, GOP, Lisbon. http://d3f5055r2rwsy1.cloudfront.net/images/cooperacao/conctestratg1420.pdf.

GOP (2009), Resolução do Conselho de Ministros No. 73/2009, GOP, Lisbon, http://dre.pt/pdf1sdip/2009/08/16500/0560305608.pdf.

IPAD (2010) *Estratégia da Cooperação Portuguesa para a Igualdade de Género,* IPAD, Lisbon, http://d3f5055r2rwsy1.cloudfront.net/images/cooperacao/estrategia_coop_iguald_genero.pdf.

IPAD (2009), *Estratégia Portuguesa de Cooperação Multilateral (*Portuguese Multilateral Co-operation Strategy*)*, IPAD, Lisbon, http://d3f5055r2rwsy1.cloudfront.net/images/cooperacao/estrategia_multilateral.pdf.

MNE/ IPAD (2006), *A Strategic Vision for Portuguese Development Cooperation*, MNE (Ministério dos Negócios Estrangeiros)/IPAD, Lisbon, http://d3f5055r2rwsy1.cloudfront.net/images/cooperacao/visao_estrategica_cp_ing.pdf.

Other sources

Davies, R. and J. Pickering (2015), "Making development co-operation fit for the future: A survey of partner countries", *OECD Development Co-operation Working Papers*, No. 20, OECD Publishing, Paris, http://dx.doi.org/10.1787/5js6b25hzv7h-en.

HLF4 (2011), "Busan Partnership for Effective Development Co-operation", HLF4 (Fourth High Level Forum on Aid Effectiveness), Busan, Korea, 29 November – 1 December, www.oecd.org/dac/effectiveness/49650173.pdf.

OECD (2012), *Recommendation of the Council on Common Approaches for Officially Supported Export Credits and Environmental and Social Due Diligence*, TAD/ECG(2012)5 28 June 2012, Trade and Agriculture Directorate, Participants to the Arrangement on Officially Supported Export Credits, OECD, Paris, http://www.oecd.org/officialdocuments/publicdisplaydocumentpdf/?cote=tad/ecg(2012)5&doclanguage=en.

OECD (2014) *Mainstreaming Cross-Cutting Issues: 7 Lessons from DAC Peer Reviews*, OECD Publishing, Paris. www.oecd.org/dac/peer-reviews/Final%20publication%20version%20of%20the%207%20Lessons%20mainstreaming%20cross%20cutting%20issues.pdf.

OECD (2011a), *OECD Development Assistance Peer Reviews: Portugal 2010*, OECD Publishing, Paris. http://dx.doi.org/10.1787/9789264098312-en.

OECD (2011b), *OECD Environmental Performance Reviews: Portugal 2011*, OECD Publishing, Paris, http://dx.doi.org/10.1787/9789264097896-en.

OECD (n.d. a), "List of fragile states and economies used for preparing the 2015 OECD report on States of Fragility", www.oecd.org/dac/governance-peace/conflictandfragility/docs/List%20of%20fragile%20states.pdf.

OECD (n.d. b), "International engagement in fragile states", www.oecd.org/dac/governance-peace/conflictandfragility/iefs.htm.

Chapter 3: Allocating Portugal's official development assistance

Overall ODA volume

Indicator: The member makes every effort to meet ODA domestic and international targets

Portugal's capacity to meet its ODA target has been compromised during the financial crisis. While it will not meet the 2015 deadline of providing 0.7% of its gross national income (GNI) as ODA, Portugal could establish an explicit plan with interim targets to meet this commitment at a later date. An additional concern is Portugal's reliance on credit lines and accompanying concessional loans. If no new lines are opened or the grant element of ODA does not increase, Portugal's aid levels could plummet when its credit lines expire or are completely drawn down by beneficiary countries.

Significant budget cuts mean Portugal will not meet its ODA volume target

Portugal will not meet its goal of allocating 0.7% of its gross national income (GNI) as ODA in 2015. Significant budget cuts made as the country passed through an Economic Adjustment Programme (see Context) have resulted in ODA falling in real terms by 19.7% since 2012 (Figure 3.1). In 2013, Portugal provided USD 488 million as ODA, or 0.23% of its GNI. The DAC average in 2013 was 0.30% (OECD, 2015a). Portugal's ODA to GNI ratio peaked in 2004, a year in which it provided significant debt relief.[1] Other than that exceptional year, ODA/GNI ratios have never surpassed 0.31% achieved in 2011.

Portugal is to be commended for maintaining its commitments to partner countries during the financial crisis. Despite the budget cuts, Camões I.P. and line ministries made efforts to maintain bilateral programmes with its six main partners. Cuts were mostly made by phasing out expiring projects and reducing or suspending core contributions to multilateral agencies where possible.

Figure 3.1 Portugal's net ODA: volume and as a share of gross national income, 1998-2013

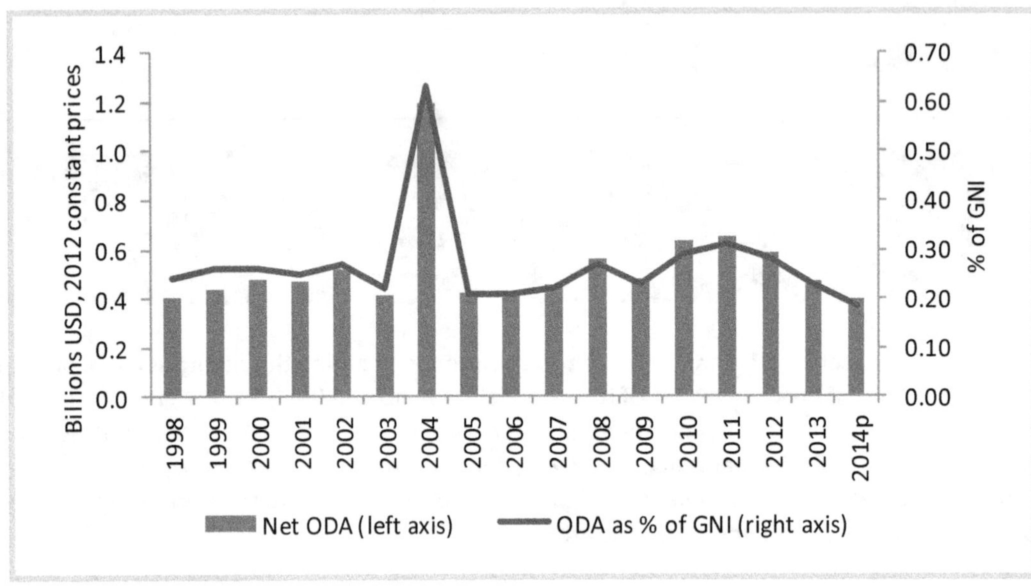

Source: OECD-DAC statistics.

Portugal's ODA budget could plummet when credit lines expire or are all spent

Portugal's heavy reliance on concessional loans to make up its ODA budget in the absence of an increase in grants has worrying implications for its ability to meet its 0.7% commitments. Since 2007 the share of ODA provided as grants has fallen, while the share provided as concessional loans has risen dramatically, from 5% of total ODA in 2006 to 41% in 2013 (Figure 3.2). Portugal has extended EUR 1.6 billion in credit since 2001 to partner countries, but as of 2015 partners had drawn down EUR 958 million (60%) of this credit in the form of loans, leaving EUR 602 million unspent (Annex D). If no new lines are opened or the grant element of ODA does not increase, aid levels could fall significantly below 0.23% of GNI to ODA, when these credit lines expire or are completely drawn down by beneficiary countries. Five of the ten credit lines have already expired and are unlikely to be renegotiated. The remaining five are due to expire no later than 2017.[2] At the time of the peer review mission, Portugal did not anticipate opening new credit lines.

To address this concern and reverse budget cuts, Portugal's government should set out a pragmatic plan to make sustainable progress towards the 0.7% GNI to ODA target. The plan should include realistic intermediary targets and set out staged increases to the grant element of its ODA budget. Since exiting the adjustment programme in 2014, Portugal's economy has shown signs of improvement (OECD 2015b). Although the country is still in post-programme surveillance, this improvement could provide impetus for Portugal to develop this plan.

In addition, Portugal should ensure that all of its ODA complies with the DAC's recommendation on the terms and conditions of aid, as proposed in the last peer review (OECD, 2011).[3] According to OECD statistics in 2013, while Portugal does now allocate 86% of its total ODA as a grant element, it is still not abiding by the recommendation to ensure at least a 90% grant element to least developed countries: in 2013, the grant element of its bilateral ODA commitments to these countries was only 84%, the lowest across the DAC.

Figure 3.2 Grants versus loans in Portuguese ODA, 2005-13

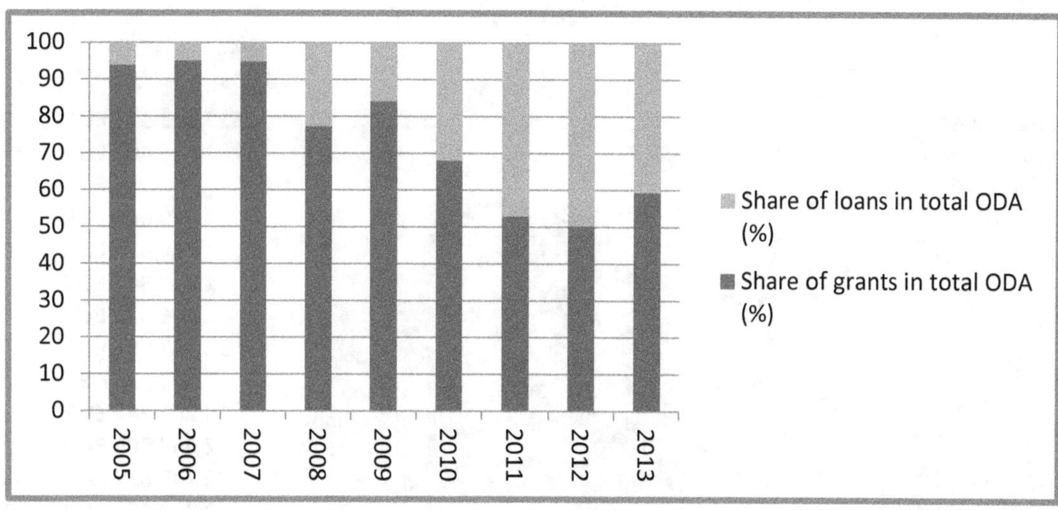

Source: OECD-DAC statistics.

Portugal's share of ODA to least developed countries is declining

Portugal has committed to increasing its total ODA funding to least developed countries through its endorsement of the 2014 OECD Development Assistance Committee's High-Level Meeting Communiqué (OECD DAC, 2014).[4] It will need to consider carefully and quickly how it distributes its ODA if it wants to meet this commitment, as its share of ODA to these countries is declining. According to OECD statistics, only 29% of its total ODA was spent on LDCs in 2013, compared to 40% on average between 2010 and 2011.[5] As a result, in 2013 it provided only 0.07% of its GNI to LDCs, far below the UN commitment of providing 0.15 – 0.20%. This decline reflects the changing status of some of Portugal's partners[6] and the increasing amount of concessional loans it has given to countries not classified as least developed.

Despite the complex development co-operation system, Camões I.P. has made great strides in ODA reporting

ODA reporting is complicated for Portugal as there is no specific state budget line for ODA; each of the 57 Portuguese public entities that implement development co-operation has their own budget for co-operation activities (Table 3.1 and Chapter 4). This makes ODA data collection and reporting difficult. Camões I.P. has, however, made great efforts at the headquarter level since the last peer review to improve its reporting practices and these have paid off. In 2015, Portugal's ODA reporting was considered excellent by the OECD secretariat (OECD, 2015c). The institute is in the process of establishing a new integrated information system that should further enhance Portugal's statistical reporting capacity (Box 6.1).

In another response to the previous peer review recommendations, Portugal is now providing four-year indicative information on spending plans to partner countries in its Indicative Cooperation Programmes and the new Strategic Cooperation Programme. Four-year figures are also reported to the OECD-DAC Forward Spending Survey (Chapter 6). The figures are subject to annual confirmation but reflect Portugal's best estimate of future aid flows, including ODA provided by other line ministries. While this involves significant effort given the fragmented nature of the system it improves predictability to partner countries.

Table 3.1 The allocation of Portugal's ODA by each line ministry, 2014 – Preliminary Data

2014		
	TOTAL	
	EUROS	%
Portuguese Government	**319 513 357 EUR**	**99.4%**
Portuguese Government (excluding MoFA)	**284 556 401 EUR**	**88.6%**
MAI-Ministry of Internal Administration	**4 419 061 EUR**	**1.4%**
MAM-Ministry of Agriculture and the Sea	**254 625 EUR**	**0.1%**
MDN-Ministry of National Defence	**1 210 341 EUR**	**0.4%**
ME-Ministry of Economy	**306 528 EUR**	**0.1%**
MEC-Ministry of Education and Science	**31 082 002 EUR**	**9.7%**
MJ-Ministry of Justice	**731 357 EU**	**0.2%**
MS-Ministry of Health	**10 267 782 EUR**	**3.2%**
MSSES-Ministry of Solidarity, Employment and Social Security	**7 065 904 EUR**	**2.2%**
MF-Ministry of Finance	**222 743 627 EUR**	**69.3%**
MAOTE-Ministry of Environment	**3 314 861 EUR**	**1.0%**
MNE-Ministry of Foreign Affairs (MoFA)	**34 956 956 EUR**	**10.9%**
Of whichCamões, IP	***23 548 027EUR***	***7.3%***
PCM-Presidency of Council Ministers	**3 160 313 EUR**	**1.0%**
Other Official Entities *(Parliament, Courts, Portuguese Central Bank, Municipalities, Regional Governments and Universities)*	**1 791 038 EUR**	**0.6%**
Portuguese Total ODA	**321 304 395 EUR**	**100%**

Source: Camões I.P. (data received on 1 July 2015).

Bilateral ODA allocations

Indicator: Aid is allocated according to the statement of intent and international commitments

Portugal's bilateral ODA allocations are consistent with its strategic plans. ODA is highly concentrated on sub-Saharan Africa where five of its six main partner countries are located. At the sector level, grant allocations are focused on social sectors and concessional loans focus mainly on infrastructure development. However, Portugal still has further to go to deliver fewer and larger projects in its bid to reduce project fragmentation.

ODA is highly concentrated on Sub-Saharan Africa and priority partner countries

Portugal's programme is highly concentrated geographically. Its priority region for development co-operation is sub-Saharan Africa, with only one main partner country in the Asia-Pacific region (Timor-Leste). Sub-Saharan Africa received 88% of Portugal's bilateral ODA allocable by region in 2013. In addition, 98 % of Portugal's bilateral country-allocable ODA went to its top 10 recipients (which include all of its partner countries). This is far above the DAC average.

ODA share to the social sectors is declining with the rise in infrastructure loans

Portugal's bilateral ODA focuses on its strategic priority sectors. Between 2012 and 2013, 37% of its bilateral ODA on average went to social infrastructure and services; 15% of this went to education alone (Figure 3.3). However, the share of its ODA allocated to social infrastructure has declined over time. Aid to the government and civil society sector in particular has fallen substantially: between 2007 and 2011, 18% of Portugal's ODA on average was allocated to this sector; between 2012 and 2013, this fell to 3%. Part of this decreasing share can be explained by the rise in Portugal's concessional loans, with over half of its bilateral ODA (52%) allocated to commodity or programme assistance. From 2007 to 2014, 70% of the credit lines and concessional loans were used to meet partner countries' road, sea and air transport infrastructure needs (Camoes I.P, 2015). It is not possible at this point to tell whether some of these loan-funded projects are supporting any of Portugal's grant investments in the social sectors.

Portugal still administers a large number of small projects in its partner countries

Portugal is aware that it still has work to do before it can deliver larger and fewer programmes, as recommended by the last peer review (OECD, 2011). The Strategic Concept (2014-2020) and new Strategic Cooperation Programmes commit Portugal to addressing this issue (Chapter 2). According to OECD statistics, it has reduced the number of projects it undertakes from an average of 900-1000 between 2006 and 2008 to an average of 713 between 2009 and 2013. However, this largely reflects the declining ODA budget, and Portugal has not yet managed to increase the financial size of its projects. In 2013 over 70% of Portugal's grant projects were valued at under USD 100 000.[7] This was also the case at the time of the last peer review.[8] All these small projects require co-ordination and take up precious administration, monitoring and evaluation capacity for Portugal and its partners. These costs could be reduced if projects were larger.

Figure 3.3 Portugal's bilateral commitments across sectors (as share of bilateral aid)

2012-13 average

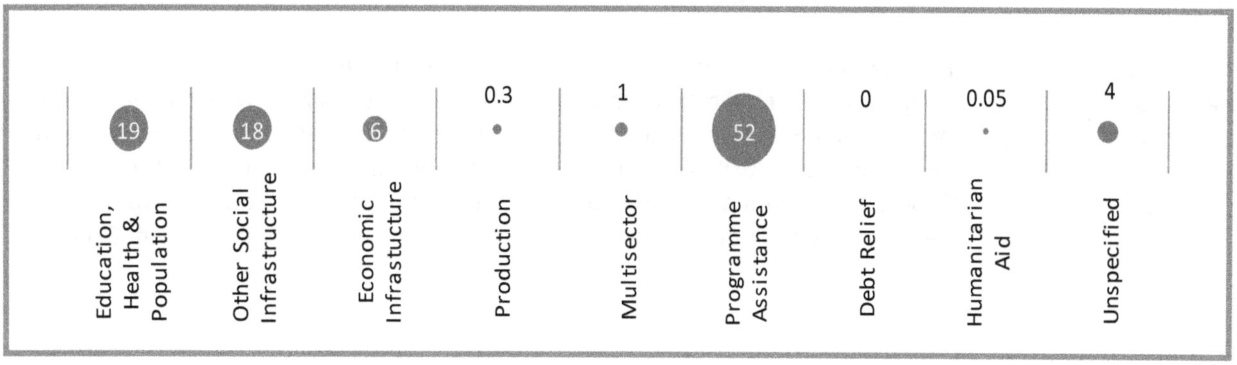

Education, Health & Population	Other Social Infrastructure	Economic Infrastucture	Production	Multisector	Programme Assistance	Debt Relief	Humanitarian Aid	Unspecified
19	18	6	0.3	1	52	0	0.05	4

Source: OECD-DAC statistics.

Multilateral ODA channel

Indicator: The member uses the multilateral aid channels effectively

Portugal has reduced its multilateral aid allocations in its efforts to recover from the financial crisis. Nonetheless, it has successfully stayed engaged at the multilateral level, actively participating in the boards of many multilateral institutions. This has been positive for Portugal and has kept open a channel through which Portugal can keep its partner countries' interests on the agendas of multilateral organisations.

Multilateral ODA has declined; the EU remains Portugal's main recipient

Multilateral engagement represents an important part of Portuguese ODA: 35% of gross disbursements in 2013. This is above the DAC average of 27%, but is less than in 2009, when the share stood at 43% (Figure 3.4; Table B.2). The declining share reflects a strategic decision by the Portuguese government, in the face of ODA budget cuts, to protect its bilateral commitments to its partner countries.

Portugal channels only 1% of its bilateral ODA to specific projects implemented by multilateral organisations in partner countries (known as multi-bi/non-core contributions). This is a relatively small share of non-core multilateral ODA compared to other DAC members.[9]

Portugal's multilateral allocations follow its strategic priorities as outlined in its multilateral strategy (IPAD, 2009). The EU institutions received about 85% of Portugal's multilateral aid in 2013. It is also one of the most important fora in which Portugal can push for its development-related interests. The UN agencies, World Bank and regional bodies like CPLP are also important multilateral partners for Portugal, though they receive significantly less aid. The CPLP brings together all Portugal's main partner countries. This reflects one of the main rationales for Portugal's engagement with multilateral organisations: that they focus on Portugal's partner countries and are active in sectors aligned with Portugal's development co-operation priorities.

Despite cuts, Portugal has maintained strategic relationships with its multilateral partners

Despite cuts to the multilateral ODA portfolio, Portugal has managed to maintain strategic multilateral relationships. For example, Portugal is currently a board member of the United Nations Development Programme (UNDP) and the United Nations Population Fund (UNFPA), and also sits on the board of the Global Fund to Fight AIDS, Tuberculosis and Malaria (The Global Fund, 2014). In 2015, Portugal also applied to become a member of the new Chinese-led Asian Infrastructure Investment Bank.

Figure 3.4 How Portugal's ODA is shared across the multilateral system, 2008-13

Gross disbursements

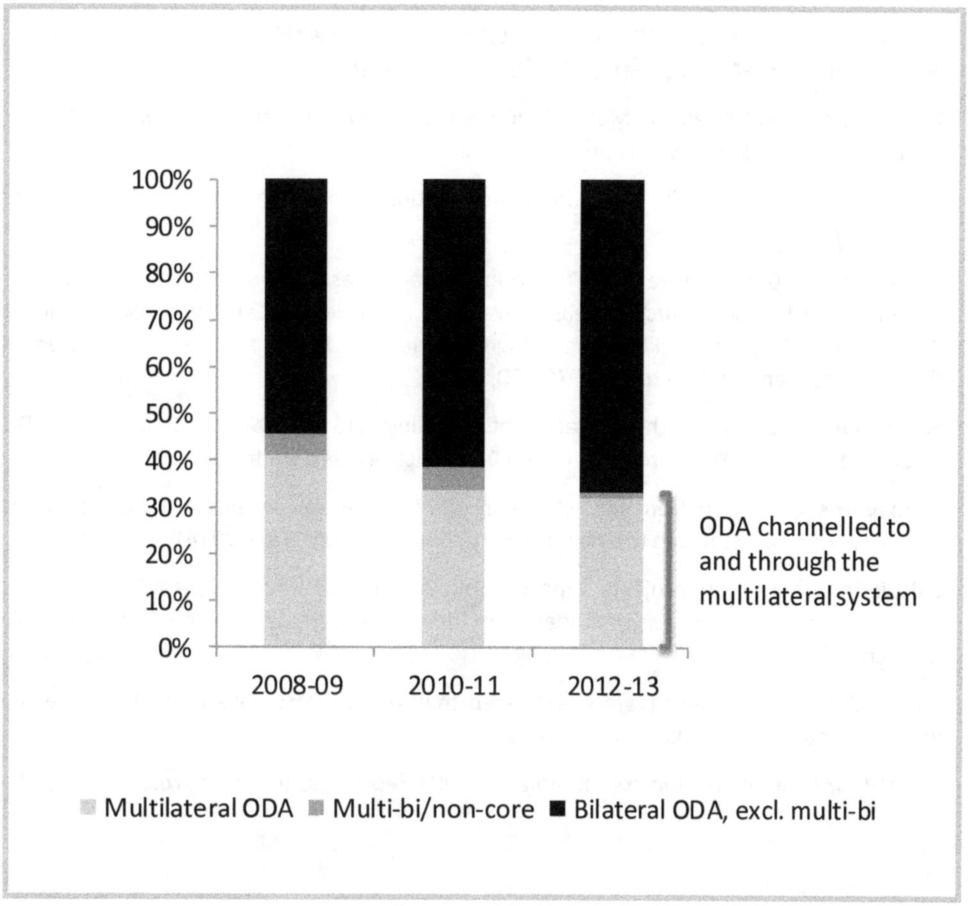

Source: OECD-DAC statistics

Notes

1. In 2004, 68% of Portugal's ODA was a result of debt relief within the framework of the Highly Indebted Poor Countries (HIPC) initiative (IPAD, n.d.) (OECD statistics).

2. Two lines of credit open for Mozambique and Cabo Verde and expiring in 2017 are currently under discussion for a possible extension.

3. For more on the DAC's 1978 Recommendations on the Terms and Conditions of Aid, see http://www.oecd.org/dac/stats/31426776.pdf.

4. In December 2014, ministers of DAC member agencies agreed to "allocate more of total ODA to countries most in need, such as least developed countries (LDCs), low-income countries, small island developing states, land-locked developing countries and fragile and conflict-affected states...reversing the declining trend of ODA to LDCs" (OECD, 2014).

5. Portugal has also not met the UN target of providing 0.15 – 0.20% of GNI as ODA to LDCs, according to OECD statistics; in 2013 it provided only 0.07% of its GNI as ODA to LDCs.

6. Cabo Verde graduated from LDC status in 2007. A UN review has also recommended that Angola graduate from LDC status in the next three to four years (UNCTAD, 2014).

7 Calculations based on projects reported by Portugal to the OECD-DAC statistical database. This calculation excludes concessional loans, as they are usually large sums and would skew the size of projects.

8. The 2010 OECD DAC peer review calculated that 70% of Portugal's projects between 2005 and 2008 were less than USD 100 000 (OECD, 2011).

9. In 2013, DAC members' non-core multilateral ODA represented 12% of gross ODA.

Bibliography

Government sources

Camões I.P. (2015), *Memorandum of Portugal*, 16 March 2015, Camões I.P. (Camões Instituto da Cooperação e da Lingua Portugal), Lisbon.

Camões I.P. (2014), *Documento de Posição de Portugal sobre a Agenda pós 2015*, Camões I.P., Lisbon.

GOP (2014), *Conceito Estratégico da Cooperação Portuguesa 2014-2020,* [Strategic Concept for Portuguese Development Cooperation 2014-2020], GOP (Government of Portugal), Lisbon. http://d3f5055r2rwsy1.cloudfront.net/images/cooperacao/conctestratg1420.pdf.

IPAD (2009), *Estratégia Portuguesa de Cooperação Multilateral* [Portuguese Multilateral Co-operation Strategy], IPAD (Instituto Português de Apoio ao Desenvolvimento), Lisbon, http://d3f5055r2rwsy1.cloudfront.net/images/cooperacao/estrategia_cooperacao_multilateral.pdf.

Other sources

European Commission (2011), "The economic adjustment programme for Portugal", *European Economy Occasional Papers,* No. 79, June 2011, Directorate General for Economic and Financial Affairs, European Commission, Brussels, http://ec.europa.eu/economy_finance/publications/occasional_paper/2011/pdf/ocp79_en.pdf.

Global Fund (2014), *Governance Handbook: Global Fund Board*, The Global Fund to Fight AIDS, Tuberculosis and Malaria, http://www.theglobalfund.org/documents/core/guides/Core_GovernanceHandbookSection4GlobalFundBoard_Handbook_en.

OECD (2015a), "Development aid stable in 2014 but flows to poorest countries still falling: Detailed summary", 8 April 2015, OECD, Paris, www.oecd.org/dac/stats/documentupload/ODA%202014%20Technical%20Note.pdf.

OECD (2015b), *Economic Outlook Volume 1*, Volume 2015 Issue 1, OECD Publishing, Paris, http://dx.doi.org/10.1787/eco_outlook-v2015-1-en.

OECD (2015c), "DAC, CRS and FSS statistical reporting issues in 2014 and 2015", DAC Working Party on Development Finance Statistics, OECD Conference Centre, Paris, 21-22 May 2015, www.oecd.org/officialdocuments/publicdisplaydocumentpdf/?cote=DCD/DAC/STAT(2015)19&docLanguage=En.

OECD (2011), *OECD Development Assistance Peer Reviews: Portugal 2010*, OECD Publishing, Paris, http://dx.doi.org/10.1787/9789264098312-en.

OECD DAC (2014), "DAC High Level Meeting: Final communiqué", DAC High Level Meeting, OECD Conference Centre, Paris, 15-16 December 2014, www.oecd.org/dac/OECD%20DAC%20HLM%20Communique.PDF.

Reuters (2 April 2015), "Portugal applies to join China-backed AIIB investment bank", Reuters, http://uk.reuters.com/article/2015/04/02/uk-asia-aiib-portugal-idUKKBN0MT06920150402.

UNCTAD (2014), *Vulnerability Profile of Angola*, UNCTAD (United Nations Conference on Trade and Development), www.un.org/en/development/desa/policy/cdp/cdp_news_archive/2015-cdp-plen-pre-5b.pdf.

Chapter 4: Managing Portugal's development co-operation

Institutional system

Indicator: The institutional structure is conducive to consistent, quality development co-operation

Portugal's current business model for delivering development co-operation is under pressure. Portugal's new development agency, Camões I.P., faces challenges in fulfilling its mandate of co-ordinating and supervising Portugal's multiple development actors. While steps have been taken since the last peer review to strengthen Camões I.P.'s coordinating powers, it does not have input into or oversight over half of Portugal's bilateral ODA budget. This was also the case for Portugal's former development agency. One factor hindering its success is constrained human and financial resources, but a more fundamental issue is whether the institute has a realistic mandate.

Portugal's business model continues to pose challenges for delivering a co-ordinated and effective programme

Portugal's complex development co-operation system, which involves 57 different public entities (Figure 3.3), each with their own ODA budget and ability to implement projects, is both an asset and a liability. While the system undoubtedly enables Portugal to draw on rich and diverse expertise from across the whole of its government, it also makes it difficult to deliver a coherent programme in partner countries.

This complex system relies on a unified vision (Chapter 2), strong co-ordination mechanisms and comprehensive quality control in order to function effectively. Under the current business model, the Secretary of State for Foreign Affairs and Co-operation is responsible at the political level for ensuring Portugal has a strategic and co-ordinated development co-operation programme. However, the day-to-day management is done by Camões I.P. (Figure 4.1), created in 2012 through a merger between Portugal's former development agency – the Portuguese Institute for Development Assistance (IPAD) – and the Camões Institute, Portugal's culture and language institute (see Context). The new institute is viewed as the "core entity" responsible for Portuguese development co-operation (GOP, 2014), alongside language and cultural promotion. Directly responsible for 7.3% of the ODA budget[1], it is tasked with proposing the "direction" of Portugal's development co-operation policy, "co-ordinating" programmes projects and activities, and having oversight of the implementation of all development co-operation programmes carried out by line ministries through audit and evaluation (GOP, 2014).

Camões I.P.'s ability to deliver its mandate is mixed. It has developed policies to guide Portugal's numerous development co-operation actors and established programme management and evaluation guidelines for these actors to use. It is also increasingly able to analyse and give its opinion on some of the line ministries' proposed programmes. However, the institute does not yet have regular input into or the ability to perform its oversight role over half of Portugal's bilateral ODA budget managed by the Ministry of Finance in the form of ODA loans. This was also a challenge for Portugal's former development agency IPAD (OECD, 2010).

Limited human and financial resources within Camões I.P. are undoubtedly one factor hindering it from delivering its objectives. The share of the ODA budget for which Camões I.P. is directly responsible has nearly halved since the last review.[2] The institute's reduced human resources are also hampering its ability to provide technical support and supervision to the line ministries.

A more fundamental issue though is whether the institute's mandate is realistic. Given the Institute's organisational set up there is a serious question as to whether Camões I.P. will ever have sufficient authority to fulfil its mandate of co-ordinating and providing oversight over Portugal's line ministries. The public institute operates outside the direct state administration[3] and has only a marginal amount of the ODA budget under its direct control, reducing its leverage over the line ministries.

The division of labour between Camões I.P. and the Ministry of Foreign Affairs is also not clear, with seemingly overlapping roles in some areas. For example, the Ministry of Foreign Affairs' Directorate for Foreign Policy is involved in reviewing the Ministry of Finance's proposed ODA loans, but at no point has the Directorate consulted with Camões I.P., despite this being part of the institute's official mandate. Formal consultation with the institute could ensure loans are better co-ordinated with existing programmes and help to integrate Portugal's cross-cutting development priorities into the projects funded by loans.

Portugal could benefit from reviewing its business model to ensure that the entity charged with managing its complex system has an appropriate mandate with sufficient capacity, as recommended in the last peer review (OECD, 2010; Annex A). As part of this review, the roles and responsibilities of Camões I.P. and the Ministry of Foreign Affairs should also be clarified – both in headquarters and in partner countries – so as to make a greater distinction between the political and technical functions of these respective institutions.

Figure 4.1 Portugal's development co-operation actors and partners

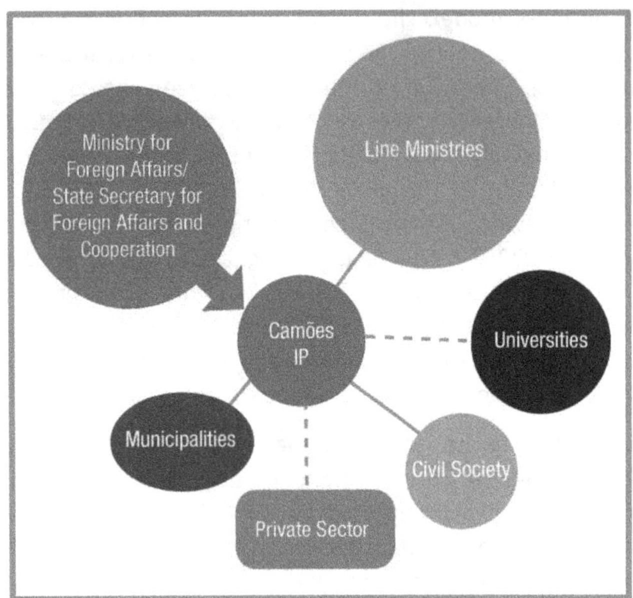

Source: Camões I.P. (2015b) *Memorandum of Portugal 2015,* Camões I.P., Lisbon, Portugal.

Co-ordination at headquarters is better, but further reforms are required

Since the last peer review, Portugal has taken steps to improve the co-ordination of development co-operation at headquarters, as recommended by the last peer review. The Inter-Ministerial Commission for Co-operation has begun to meet at the political level and approves the line ministries' annual development plans. Camões I.P.'s role of providing a "prior opinion" on projects proposed by line ministries has also been made legally binding. The institute has good informal links with many of the ministries who rely on it for advice, and it has been able to intervene early on in the design phase of some line ministries' projects, using its development expertise to enhance impact.[4] It has also helped those municipalities that deliver development co-operation to establish a network to share their experiences and enhance co-ordination, as recommended.

However, despite these reforms, co-ordination still remains an issue. The commission meets only twice a year at the political level and there is no mechanism in place to enable the commission to ensure there is harmonisation between Portugal's Strategic Cooperation Programmes for partner countries and the line ministries' development co-operation plans. Humanitarian response, which technically should be co-ordinated by Camões I.P., is in reality co-ordinated through the Ministry of Interior (Chapter 7). In addition, while Portugal's former development agency was involved in giving input into the establishment of the credit lines managed by the Ministry of Finance, Camões I.P. has not given its prior opinion on any of the individual projects funded from these credit lines, nor has it so far seen or participated in any evaluations of these projects to assess their development impact (Chapter 6).

Strong whole-of-government presence in partner countries, but harmonisation can be an issue

Portugal has a strong whole-of-government presence in its partner countries, with many line ministries (Justice, Defence, International Affairs) having their own representatives in-country. This has enabled Portugal to exploit synergies across the various policy communities and to deliver a comprehensive approach to development, beyond ODA, as evidenced in Sao Tome and Principe (Annex C and see Box 4.1).

However, this strong whole-of-government presence can also make harmonisation complicated, particularly given that many line ministries have their own direct relationships with their counterparts in partner countries. The joint expert mission to Guinea-Bissau in 2014 (Box 4.1) is a good example of an integrated response to partner country programming that could be emulated in other countries to ensure a truly co-ordinated approach on the ground.

Box 4.1 A whole-of-government approach in Guinea-Bissau

In September 2014 Portugal undertook a whole-of-government mission to Guinea-Bissau to explore how to resume its institutional co-operation with the government, which had been interrupted by a *coup d'état* in April 2012. The mission was led by Camões I.P. and the Directorate-General for Foreign Policy. Six other line ministries participated: education, agriculture, justice, employment and social security, environment and spatial planning and internal affairs. By bringing all the actors together to discuss with the Guinea-Bissau government its needs, Portugal has been able to deliver a more integrated and harmonised response.

Source: Camões I.P. (2015b) *Memorandum of Portugal 2015,* Camões I.P., Lisbon, Portugal.

An ambitious systems reform is taking place

Camões I.P. is making efforts to strengthen its programme management procedures and is putting in place a risk and quality management system, a results-based management process and an integrated financial information system (Chapter 6). While there is undoubtedly a need to improve processes, management should reflect on whether the institute has the capacity to undertake this ambitious agenda and if the new systems and procedures can be applied easily to all of Portugal's development actors.

Portugal has taken steps to decentralise its operations, but there is further to go

Since the last peer review, Portugal has made progress in decentralising its co-operation, in line with the recommendations (OECD, 2010). The Ministry of Foreign Affairs and Camões I.P. have increased the share of their development staff in the field from 12% in 2008 to 32% in 2012 (OECD, 2014).[5] Embassies are also more engaged, having a greater input into programme design and monitoring.

There is scope, though, to decentralise further. Embassies still have very little financial authority, as observed in Sao Tome and Principe (Annex C). Efforts underway to enable Embassies to have greater financial authority should be intensified as more robust processes are put in place to improve oversight from headquarters. Portugal could also make better use of existing staff, particularly line ministry staff posted in partner countries, which tend to focus exclusively on their given projects. Finally, Portugal could also use local staff in partner countries: in Sao Tome and Principe, for example, no local staff were employed in the embassy to cover development co-operation exclusively.

Adaptation to change

Indicator: The system is able to reform and innovate to meet evolving needs

Portugal's development co-operation system has undergone significant changes since the last peer review. It is too soon to assess the impact of the merger of Portugal's former development agency, IPAD, with Portugal's culture and language institute on its ability to carry out effective development co-operation. However, the newly formed Camões I.P. should be commended for maintaining delivery to key partners during the transition. While efficiencies have been made, the reform has not yet fully resolved some of the major challenges of co-ordination that afflicted Portugal's former development agency nor is it clear that the merger has enhanced the impact of Portugal's development co-operation as hoped. There is also no system in place to encourage innovation.

Camões I.P. has focused on maintaining delivery to key partners during a turbulent period of reform

Portugal's development co-operation system has gone through a turbulent period of change since the last peer review, with ODA budget cuts, structural reforms and a succession of leadership changes.[6] The 2012 merger of Camões Institute and IPAD was driven by an extensive government-wide public administration reform process (see Context) and was aimed primarily at achieving efficiencies. However, it was also viewed by some as a 'good fit' that could ultimately enhance Portugal's development co-operation impact, given that the two organisations often work in similar partner countries and undertake some joint programmes.

A recent staff survey showed that over half of respondents were satisfied with the way management has handled the organisational reform process (Camões I.P., 2015a). Camões I.P. should also be commended for successfully maintaining delivery to key partners during the transition, thereby minimising risks.

While it is too soon to assess fully the impact of the merger, it is clear that the reform has helped to achieve efficiencies through joint support and management functions, and shared offices in the field and at headquarters. There is still further to go, though, in terms of forming a unified internal organisational culture and a recognisable public identity associated not just with culture and language, but also with development co-operation (Chapter 6). The reform has also not resolved the challenges that afflicted Portugal's former development agency. These centred on the lack of capacity and authority to co-ordinate and supervise the implementation of all of Portugal's development co-operation programmes.

Portugal should appraise whether the merger has enhanced the development impact of its co-operation as hoped. The appraisal should pay special attention to whether the Institute has been successful in ensuring that language instruction and cultural promotion, when funded by ODA, are only used to promote development, as recommended by the last peer review.

Limited culture of innovation

While Portugal is aware of the importance of fostering innovation (GOP, 2014) it does not yet have incentives in place to encourage the multiple actors working on development co-operation to take risks and pilot new approaches. The process of decentralisation to the field should create opportunities for promoting innovation.

Human resources

Indicator: The member manages its human resources effectively to respond to field imperatives

Human resource management is a challenge for Camões I.P. A constrained budget, and inflexible recruitment procedures are hampering its ability to bring in, rotate and retain the skills it requires to manage an effective development programme. Given the restrictions it faces to recruit staff, it could review delegated authority in headquarters as well as the field to ensure staff are being empowered, assess whether it has the right skills in the right places, and think creatively about filling skills gaps.

Rigid recruitment procedures continue to hamper effective human resource management

Since the last peer review, the number of staff working on development co-operation within Portugal's development agency (IPAD/Camões I.P.) has fallen. Staff numbers in Portugal's former development agency, IPAD, were cut from 152 in 2010 to 137 in 2012. The merger of IPAD with the Camões Institute resulted in a further loss of 19 staff across both organisations. Fiscal consolidation and structural reform in response to Portugal's economic crisis have been critical factors behind this decline, with the ODA budget declining and government-wide public sector reforms reducing and restructuring the public sector workforce.

Against this backdrop, the institute's annual budget allocated to human resources has been until recently insufficient to cover all the posts that were agreed in its establishment plan (Camões I.P., 2015b). At the time of this peer review, the Development Cooperation Directorate, for example, has five unfilled posts and lacks dedicated staff to manage its humanitarian aid or to ensure gender is integrated into programming.

Portugal's rigid recruitment procedures also impose considerable constraints. While Camões I.P. staff are now able to rotate from headquarters to the field – something they were not able to do in the last peer review - the institute is still unable to hire staff with specialist development expertise at headquarters. Specialists can be recruited in partner countries, but only for fixed term contracts. These procedures hamper Camões I.P.'s ability to bring in and retain the skills it requires.

Given these constraints, Camões I.P. could benefit from reviewing delegated authority in headquarters as well as the field to ensure decisions are taken at the appropriate levels. The institute should also consider undertaking an organisation-wide skills assessment to see whether it has the right skills in the right places for maximising its human resources. In addition, there is scope to think more innovatively about how to fill skills gaps. The institute's recent internship programme with Calouste Gulbenkian Foundation provides a good example of creative thinking. The foundation regularly pays for trainees to work in Camões I.P., providing the institute with greater staff capacity at limited costs to its budget.

Camões I.P. is putting in place a more strategic approach to staff training

Camões I.P.'s new integrated training plan links staff training to the institute's overall corporate objectives (Camões I.P., 2014). During 2013 - 14 staff from the development co-operation area of the institute took part in 11 training events covering a wide range of areas, including project cycle management and civil crisis management. Camões I.P.'s staff survey found that the majority of respondents were satisfied with senior management's promotion of training and enthusiastic about participating in training and taking on new working methods (Camões I.P., 2015a).

Notes

1. In 2014 Camões I.P.'s ODA budget amounted to EUR 23.5 million, representing 7.3% of Portuguese ODA.

2. It was responsible for just under 15% of the ODA budget in 2010, according to the last OECD peer review (OECD, 2011).

3. Camões I.P. has its own administrative and financial autonomy and its own assets. It performs duties which fall under the responsibility of the Ministry of Foreign Affairs (MFA).

4. A representative from the Ministry of Education cited an example of this during the peer review's mission trip to Lisbon. Camões I.P. proposed amendments to the ministry's project to ensure it was better aligned with Timor-Leste's national education system. The suggestions were taken on board and the project was adapted.

5. Portugal has a Cooperation Attaché in each of its partner countries. This post is recruited and paid for by the Ministry of Foreign Affairs, and reports to Camões I.P. and the Ambassador. The Attachés are responsible for co-ordinating co-operation in the field. Portugal also has co-operation agents in the field who are hired by Camões I.P. and who provide technical support. The increase in staff has come from Camões I.P. placing more co-operation agents in its partner countries. In 2010 it had 10 agents in the field - in 2015 it had 40.

6. Since the last peer review there have been three different Secretaries of State for Foreign Affairs and Cooperation.

Bibliography

Government sources

Camões I.P. (2015a), *Questionario de Satisfação Interna 2014, Gabinete de Avaliação e Auditoria* [Internal Satisfaction Questionnaire 2014, Evaluation and Audit Office], Camões I.P. (Camões Instituto da Cooperação e da Lingua Portugal), Lisbon, Portugal.

Camões I.P. (2015b), *Memorandum of Portugal 2015*, Camões I.P., Lisbon, Portugal.

Camões I.P. (2014), *Plano Estratégico de Formação Integrada do Camões I.P. (PeFi)*, Camões I.P., Lisbon, Portugal.

GOP (2014), *Conceito Estratégico da Cooperação Portuguesa 2014-2020* [Strategic Concept for Portuguese Development Cooperation 2014-2020], GOP (Government of Portugal), Lisbon. http://d3f5055r2rwsy1.cloudfront.net/images/cooperacao/conctestratg1420.pdf.

Other sources

OECD (2010), *OECD Development Assistance Peer Reviews: Portugal 2010*, OECD Publishing, Paris, http://dx.doi.org/10.1787/9789264098312-en.

Portuguese NGDO Platform (forthcoming), *DAC/OECD 2015 Peer Review to Portuguese Development Cooperation*, Portuguese Platform, Lisbon.

Chapter 5: Portugal's development co-operation delivery and partnerships

Budgeting and programming processes

Indicator: These processes support quality aid as defined in Busan

Portugal's progress towards meeting its international aid effectiveness commitments is mixed. It has improved multi-annual predictability and strengthened risk management since the last review. However, it is finding it a challenge to use country systems and its share of tied aid remains extremely high.

Predictability is better, but flexibility remains a problem

Portugal's changes to its state budget process since the last peer review allow it to provide its partners with more predictable, long-term funding.[1] As a result, it's new Strategic Cooperation Programmes with partner countries include indicative financial envelopes for each sector of intervention, spanning the next four to five years.

Flexibility, however, remains a problem. Portugal has limited ability to transfer ODA funds within and across countries in response to partners' changing needs. This is a result of its lack of a single unified ODA budget and the fact that each line ministry has its own ODA budget. Portugal's response to the *coup d'état* in Guinea-Bissau in April 2012, though, does show that flexibility is possible. While Portugal suspended its institutional co-operation with the Government of Guinea-Bissau, it was able to re-direct its ODA to projects implemented by civil society or multilateral organisations in order to maintain support to the country.

Programmes are aligned and there is strong country ownership

Portugal remains firmly committed to the principle of country ownership of the development process (GOP, 2014). Partner country governments are, where possible, involved in the design, monitoring and evaluation of country programmes, as the peer review observed in Sao Tome and Principe (Annex C). This results in Portugal's programmes being highly aligned with country priorities.

Portugal is still struggling to make better use of country systems and move beyond project approaches

While Portugal is committed to making better use of country systems in partner countries (GOP, 2014) only 23% of Portugal's aid to the government sector being delivered through partner's public finance and procurements systems in 2013 (OECD/UNDP, 2014. This is far below the international aid effectiveness target of 57% by 2015. Portugal is aware, though, of the need to build partners' capacity in this area to improve their systems. In 2012 it implemented 116 projects focused on strengthening governance, institutions and public finance management processes in partner countries (GOP, 2015).

Portugal is also keen to use a wider variety of aid modalities to implement its co-operation and has committed to deploy a greater mix of project aid, budget support and technical assistance in partner countries (GOP, 2014), as recommended in the last peer review. Since the last peer review, it has managed to reduce the share of its aid provided as technical assistance.[2] However, it still provides the vast majority of its aid through project-based approaches (55% of total ODA in 2013) and only a marginal amount through sector and general budget support mechanisms (1% in 2013).[3]

For Portugal to improve its use of country systems and use a wider variety of aid modalities, there is a need for stronger guidance and better use of existing staff to engage with these processes.

Steps taken to improve risk management, including tackling corruption

Since the last review, Camões I.P. has strengthened its approach to risk, establishing a risk management committee and policy. The policy identifies several types of risks and assigns key personnel with the responsibility for monitoring them within the organisation (Camões I.P., 2015). The institute has also introduced risk matrixes for projects. These encourage all project managers in Camões I.P. and across the line ministries to identify, weigh and monitor risks (Camões I.P., n.d.).[4] Risks are not, however, systematically identified or monitored at the country programme level. Camões I.P. hopes to address this gap through its new Strategic Cooperation Programmes (Camões I.P., 2015).

Camões I.P. has taken considerable steps to improve the way it addresses corruption in its programming. It has established a reporting mechanism for staff that suspect corruption and is starting to cross-check the companies with which it conducts business against debarment lists published by multilateral development agencies. Other line ministries are partnering with the United Nations Office on Drugs and Crime (UNODC) to provide training in corruption investigation and prosecution for judges and magistrates in Portugal's partner countries. After a critical review in 2013 (OECD, 2013) of the country's performance in implementing the OECD Convention on Combating Bribery of Foreign Public Officials in International Business Transactions, Portugal does appear to have made some progress in this area (Chapter 1).

Levels of tied aid are very high

In 2013 70% of Portugal's bilateral ODA was tied according to OECD statistics. This is far above the DAC average (14.3%) and represents a significant increase from the last peer review.[5] In this respect, Portugal has not met the recommendation in the 2010 peer review. High levels of tied aid not only go against Portugal's Busan development effectiveness commitments to accelerate efforts to untie aid (HLF4, 2011).

Portugal's tied aid remains high as a result of the Ministry of Finance's credit lines, which are legally tied to the purchase of Portuguese goods and services. While Portugal is not, at present, issuing any new credit lines, partners had not accessed all the funds available to them as of July 2015 (Chapter 3 and Annex D). In the absence of a sharp increase in ODA grants, Portugal is likely to continue to have a high share of tied aid.

Conditions are agreed jointly

Portugal attaches conditions to its budget support, drawing on jointly agreed conditions with partner governments, where possible.[6]

Partnerships

Indicator: The member makes appropriate use of co-ordination arrangements, promotes strategic partnerships to develop synergies, and enhances mutual accountability

Portugal has increased its involvement in country-led co-ordination processes since the last peer review. It continues to undertake delegated programming on behalf of other providers and is engaged in triangular co operation. It also actively practices mutual accountability with its partner countries. However, Portugal is still working on developing strategic framework relationships with its NGO partners and has only partially met the recommendation in the last peer review on this regard.

Portugal is more involved in country-led co ordination mechanisms

Portugal has actively increased its engagement in country-led co-ordination mechanisms since the last peer review. In Cabo Verde it is joint co-ordinator of the budget support group on security, along with the EU. In Sao Tome and Principe it is working with UNDP to establish an aid co-ordination unit. Greater engagement in country-led co-ordination mechanisms has been possible since Portugal posted more staff to the field. For example, in order to participate more actively in the donor co-ordination group in Mozambique - the G19[7] - Portugal increased its field staff.

Portugal is also continuing to undertake delegated programming on behalf of other donors. It has implemented delegated co-operation projects in Mozambique and Timor-Leste and is in the final stages of negotiating new delegated projects in Guinea-Bissau and Timor-Leste.

Portugal practices mutual accountability

Portugal reported in 2015 to the EU that it is involved in mutual accountability arrangements in 80% of its partner countries (GOP, 2015). It sees its country programmes very much as a joint endeavour with its partner country governments. All country programmes are co-signed and partners are invited at the end of the programme to participate in a joint evaluation (Chapter 6) in which they can either praise or criticise Portugal's performance.[8]

Prudent approach to working more with the private sector; further triangular co-operation planned

Portugal's Strategic Concept calls for the need to work with a wider array of development actors to deliver co-operation, including the private sector (GOP, 2014). There certainly is an opportunity for Portugal to engage further with this sector, given the heavy presence of Portuguese companies in many partner countries. In Sao Tome and Principe alone 530 Portuguese companies provide services and goods to the country. However, Camões I.P. does not currently have expertise on this issue and has prudently decided to put on hold establishing a private sector policy until it has greater capacity (Chapter 1).

Portugal is a key advocate of triangulate co-operation, jointly hosting with the OECD a policy dialogue on triangular co-operation in May 2013 in Lisbon.[9] Camões I.P. is in the midst of preparing new triangular programmes with Chile in Mozambique, and with Japan in Guinea-Bissau and Sao Tome and Principe, respectively.

Portugal is keen to develop strategic multi-annual partnerships with its NGO partners

Portugal recognises civil society as a key partner in development co-operation (GOP, 2015) with a role to play in policy consultation, project implementation and development awareness. The overall amount of funding to civil society organisations has declined since the last peer review in terms of volume, but remains a small but stable share of overall ODA.[10]

Since the last peer review, Camões I.P. has established multi-year funding relationships with several of its NGO partners. It has not yet, however, managed to move from project based funding relationships to strategic framework agreements that support NGOs' entire set of programmes. As a result it has only partially met the recommendation in the 2010 peer review (OECD, 2011).[11]The institute does intend to establish these partnerships in the near future. These partnerships could reduce transaction costs and enable Portugal to engage in deeper and more flexible relationships with NGOs.

There is also scope for Camões I.P. to streamline its project-based civil society funding mechanisms. Many Portuguese civil society organisations highlighted the high transaction costs they face, relative to other donors, in accessing funding from the institute (Annex C). They proposed that the institute consider adopting a two-step application process, which would enable them to submit short concept proposals and then, if there is interest, a more detailed proposal. This would reduce transaction costs. Portugal could also improve the predictability of its funding to humanitarian NGOs (Chapter 7).

Fragile states

Indicator: Delivery modalities and partnerships help deliver quality results in fragile contexts

Portugal has a pragmatic, flexible approach to working in fragile states. There is strong commitment to working with government-led co-ordination mechanisms and to promoting security and development issues on the global stage. Closer collaboration across government, perhaps through shared risk and context analyses, could help build greater synergies among programmes and help ensure that Portugal builds on its past experiences in individual fragile contexts.

Need for closer collaboration across government, perhaps through shared risk and context analyses

The 2010 peer review recommended that Portugal raise awareness of the "do no harm" principle, and the importance of conflict sensitivity when programming in fragile contexts (OECD, 2011). This has been done. The root causes of insecurity appear to be well understood across government programming. There is a strong focus on technical military co-operation, given Portugal's understanding of the role played by the military in the stabilisation (and destabilisation) of fragile contexts, and the Ministry of Defence ensures that a focus on the Rule of Law is part of this work. There is also a clear understanding across government that results take time in fragile states, and that flexibility needs to be built into programmes to allow for unexpected changes in context.

The 2010 review also recommended that Portugal should engage in joint analyses and use the findings to inform country programming. Here the review team found that more could be done; closer collaboration across government throughout the programme cycle, perhaps around a shared context and risk analysis, could help Portugal better capitalise on past experiences, promote coherent approaches to risk management and create greater synergies between programmes. While contextual risks are assessed in individual programme documents and strategic programmes, Portugal is missing the opportunity to reduce these risks by joining up all its efforts in a fragile state.

Portugal is proactively engaging with government-led donor co-ordination mechanisms

Portugal actively engages with government-led donor co-ordination mechanisms, where these exist, in fragile states. For example, in Timor-Leste, Portugal works with the donor support group and Timor-Leste Transparency Portal and has aligned its new country strategy, covering 2014-17, with Timor-Leste's own strategic plan.[12] There is also direct co-ordination with other development partners: in Timor-Leste the majority of funds is sourced as delegated co-operation from the EU, for example. Portugal also seeks to collaborate with other donors on the international stage. In July 2015 it hosted a high-level mission to Guinea Bissau with the DAC Chair in an attempt to promote support for the principles of the New Deal for Fragile States in that country.

A pragmatic, flexible approach to working in fragile states

Portugal has a pragmatic, flexible approach to working in fragile states; this has included adapting its programming tools when necessary. For example, Portugal is not required to use country systems by default in fragile states and it can also fund national NGOs. Flexible use of funds is also considered important; when Guinea Bissau experienced political turmoil in 2012, Portugal was able to remain engaged by withdrawing from institutional co-operation and instead executing those programmes through NGOs; this is good practice.

Notes

1. While Portugal's state budget continues to be determined on an annual basis, the introduction of a multi-annual framework for state budget planning (over at least three years) enables it to provide multi-annual indicative budgets to its partners for each sector.

2. The share of Portugal's net ODA that is provided as technical assistance has declined steeply since the last peer review according to OECD statistics. In 2009 free standing technical assistance made up 28% of total net ODA; in 2013 it made up only 14%. This partly reflects the significant decline in the grant share of Portugal's ODA over this period.

3. In 2013 Portugal was providing general and sector budget support in Mozambique and sector budget support to Cabo Verde.

4. For example, the project document for Portugal's major health programme conducted in Sao Tome and Principe provides some indication of events that could negatively affect the project: "Risks and unforeseen circumstances" identified include: no disbursement of co-financing tranches; lack of water and electricity provision; no political will from authorities in Sao Tome and Principe to implement the health sector strategy and delays in the delivery of equipment to the country (IPAD, n.d.).

5. In 2009, 38.8% of Portugal's bilateral ODA was tied.

6. Portugal's General Budget Support to Cabo Verde is tied to macroeconomic stability, effective implementation of public finance reforms, and progress made on achieving Cabo Verde's Growth and Poverty Reduction Strategy III 2012-16.

7. This group represents those donors that contribute over 30% of Mozambique's total state budget and is intended to maintain continuity of dialogue with the Mozambican authorities.

8. For example, Portugal has undertaken a Joint Evaluation of its Indicative Cooperation Programmes in Mozambique, Cabo Verde, Timor-Leste and Angola since the last peer review.

9. For more information on this policy dialogue please see the page on "Policy dialogue on triangular co-operation" on the OECD website, www.oecd.org/dac/dac-global-relations/dialogue-triangular-cooperation.htm.

10. Portugal provided only 3% of its total net ODA to and through NGOs in 2013 according to OECD statistics, below the DAC average of 13%. While the amount of ODA to and through NGOs has declined since 2010, as a result of the falling aid budget, the share has remained the same.

11. In light of declining flows to NGOs, Camões I.P. has introduced new co-financing requirements for some of its funding to NGOs which give preference to projects with guaranteed international co-financing. The rationale for these new criteria is to enable Camões I.P. to leverage greater flows and to encourage Portuguese NGOs to seek new funding models in a context of limited finances. However, civil society organisations in Portugal feel that these changes have unintentionally penalised smaller NGOs, which have less access to international funding than their larger counterparts (ONGD, 2015).

12. See Timor-Leste's Strategic Plan for 2011-30 (Democratic Republic of Timor-Leste, 2011).

Bibliography

Government sources

Camões I.P. (2015), *Memorandum of Portugal 2015*, Camões I.P. (Camões Instituto da Cooperação e da Lingua Portugal), Lisbon, Portugal.

Camões I.P. (2014), *Fórum da Cooperação para o Desenvolvimento: Regulamento* [Co-operation Forum for Development: Regulation], Camões I.P., Lisbon, Portugal, http://d3f5055r2rwsy1.cloudfront.net/images/cooperacao/reg_fcd2014.pdf.

Camões I.P. (n.d. a), *Apresentação de Propostas de Programas, Projetos ou Ações de Cooperação para o Desenvolvimento: Instruções de Preenchimento*, Camões I.P., Lisbon, Portugal. http://d3f5055r2rwsy1.cloudfront.net/images/cooperacao/formulario_apres_ppa_instrucoes.pdf.

Camões I.P. (n.d. b), *Ações Implemntadas: Paris a Busan* [Action Plan: Paris to Busan], http://www.instituto-camoes.pt/eficacia-da-ajuda/root/cooperacao/cooperacao-para-desenvolvimento/eficacia-da-ajuda, accessed 29 June 2015.

GOP (2015), "Government of Portugal's response to the EU Accountability Report - Questionnaire 2015", unpublished, GOP (Government of Portugal), Lisbon.

GOP (2014), *Conceito Estratégico da Cooperação Portuguesa 2014-2020,* [Strategic Concept for Portuguese Development Cooperation 2014-2020], GOP (Government of Portugal), Lisbon. http://d3f5055r2rwsy1.cloudfront.net/images/cooperacao/conctestratg1420.pdf

IPAD (2009), Portuguese Action Plan on Aid Effectiveness (from Paris to Accra): Summary, IPAD (Instituto Português de Apoio ao Desenvolvimento), Lisbon, http://d3f5055r2rwsy1.cloudfront.net/images/cooperacao/plano_accao_parisacra_summary.pdf.

Other sources

Democratic Republic of Timor-Leste (2011), *Timor-Leste Strategic Development Plan 2011-2030*, Democratic Republic of Timor-Leste, http://timor-leste.gov.tl/wp-content/uploads/2011/07/Timor-Leste-Strategic-Plan-2011-20301.pdf.

Government of Cabo Verde (2012), *Estratégia de Crescimento e de Redução da Pobreza III 2012–2016* [Growth and Poverty Reduction Strategy III 2012-2016], Government of Cabo Verde, Praia.

HLF3 (2008), "Accra Agenda for Action", in *The Paris Declaration on Aid Effectiveness and the Accra Agenda for Action,* Third High Level Forum on Aid Effectiveness, www.oecd.org/dac/effectiveness/34428351.pdf.

HLF4 (2011), "Busan Partnership for Effective Development Co-operation", HLF4 (Fourth High Level Forum on Aid Effectiveness), Busan, Korea, 29 November – 1 December, www.oecd.org/dac/effectiveness/49650173.pdf.

OECD (2013), *Phase 3 Report on Implementing the OECD Anti-Bribery Convention in Portugal*, OECD Publishing, Paris, www.oecd.org/daf/anti-bribery/Portugalphase3reportEN.pdf.

OECD (2011), *OECD Development Assistance Peer Reviews: Portugal 2010*, OECD Publishing, Paris, http://dx.doi.org/10.1787/9789264098312-en.

OECD/UNDP (2014), *Making Development Co-operation More Effective: 2014 Progress Report*, OECD Publishing, Paris, http://dx.doi.org/10.1787/9789264209305-en.

Chapter 6: Results management and accountability of Portugal's development co-operation

Results-based management system

Indicator: A results-based management system is in place to assess performance on the basis of development priorities, objectives and systems of partner countries

Camões I.P. is putting in place a results-based management system. Results are already identified at the project level and Camões I.P. is beginning to develop them for its country programmes. At this stage, project and country level results are limited to capturing outputs. Putting in place a set of measurable results at the country level which also capture outcomes and impact will enable the institute to assess the performance of Portugal's ODA. Monitoring is still work in progress given Portugal's fragmented aid system and partner country data are scarcely used.

Results-based management for projects is better, but the system lacks a results culture

Portugal emphasises that accountability and learning are central concerns for development co-operation amid a government-wide push for more performance-based public sector management. Since the last review, Camões I.P. has introduced a requirement that all project proposals – submitted by line ministries for prior opinion and from civil society organisations[1] for funding – must include a logical framework. This is still a work in progress. A sample of project documents analysed shows that some are more thoroughly prepared than others and that all projects only consider results at the output level.

Portugal's new Strategic Cooperation Programmes are beginning to be rolled out across partner countries. These include objectives and indicators for measuring progress at the country level and apply to all Portuguese actors involved in co-operation activities in that country. For example, the new Strategic Cooperation Programme for Timor-Leste 2014-2017 aligns Portuguese projects and activities to the specific goals and objectives expressed by the East Timorese government in its Strategic Development Plan 2011-2030. However, results are still expressed in terms of outputs instead of outcomes (Camões I.P. 2014a).

Portugal still has some way to go to be able to capture the development outcomes and impacts of its projects and programmes in the countries and regions in which it works. Ensuring all country programmes have a clear set of outcome-orientated results will improve the institute's ability to assess ODA projects within these countries and could help the institute and Portugal's other development actors to adjust their project designs, where needed, to ensure greater impact.

Results tracking across the development co-operation system is challenging; use of partner country data is limited

Camões I.P. is grappling with how to ensure results monitoring that is high quality and harmonised across the entire development co-operation system. A key challenge is changing the focus of project monitoring from reporting on whether project deadlines have been met and financial targets kept, to measuring progress against output and outcome results. In order to help this transition, Camões I.P. plans to prepare guidelines to help all co-operation actors when monitoring results. Portugal also needs to ensure management routinely uses results data to inform decision making and programme design.

Using partner country data in monitoring continues to be a challenge for Portugal. Use of these data is still very limited, due to lack of experience and the dearth of data collected by partner country governments.

Evaluation system

Indicator: The evaluation system is in line with the DAC evaluation principles

Camões I.P. has a well-developed evaluation system, but there is scope to improve line ministries' evaluation practices to ensure a consistent standard. The Evaluation and Audit Division in Camões I.P. is independent of the operations unit and has a clear policy and plan to guide its work. While the number of staff has increased, the division's workload has also considerably expanded. Portugal includes partner countries in its evaluation process, which is good practice.

Evaluation is well-structured at Camões I.P.

Evaluation is a well-established part of Camões I.P.'s development co-operation programme cycle and is supported by a strong set of guidance and quality control measures. For example, to ensure the quality of evaluations Camões I.P. appoints a management group for each evaluation and a matrix for assessing the quality is created for each evaluation report (Camões I.P., 2015). However, there is still further to go to ensure an evaluation culture across all of Portugal's development actors. In particular, there appears to have been no evaluation to date by the Portuguese government of its extensive concessional loan portfolio managed by the Ministry of Finance, though one is planned.

Steps are being taken to try to improve this situation. A new evaluation policy for Camões I.P. was at a draft stage during this peer review (Camões I.P. n.d.). It takes into account standards agreed by the OECD DAC (OECD, 2010) and grants the Institute's Evaluation and Audit Division a clear mandate to evaluate all development co-operation interventions and to ensure the quality of evaluations conducted by other line ministries. The draft evaluation policy has been discussed with line ministries in an effort to increase the uptake of the policy by all Portuguese development actors. Camões I.P. is also offering training to line ministries on evaluation.

While staffing numbers have been increased within Camões I.P.'s Audit and Evaluation Division,[2] the division's workload has also expanded as a result of the merger.[3] The division is keen for some of its responsibilities – such as assisting with project monitoring – to be done by staff based in partner countries. This makes sense as staff on the ground are closer to programming and have local knowledge. This would free up the division to focus on larger evaluations and its other responsibilities.

Camões I.P.'s Evaluation and Audit Division is independent of operations

The Evaluation and Audit Unit reports directly to the board of Camões I.P. and is independent of operations. The division proposes a work plan which is approved by the board at Camões I.P. Final evaluation reports are published only after a discussion with all interested parties (NGOs, partner country representatives etc.).

Camões I.P. has a strategic and comprehensive evaluation plan

Camões I.P. has a rolling three-year evaluation plan approved by the institute's senior management.[4] The 2014-16 plan is strategic, for example, it will assess the effectiveness of Camões I.P.'s new NGO co-financing mechanism and, it will, for the first time, evaluate an infrastructure loan project funded by Portugal's credit line.[5]

The plan does not specify the financial allocation for each exercise and there is no dedicated budget for evaluation. However, staff interviewed in the Evaluation and Audit Unit informed that the budget attached to evaluations in 2015 was EUR 100 000, excluding salaries.

Evaluation partnerships between Portugal and partner countries are positive

Camões I.P. strives to include partner countries in the evaluation cycle. Terms of reference are drafted with staff of partner country embassies in Lisbon as well as other stakeholders in partner countries. They are also invited to participate throughout the process on the ground. The involvement of partner countries does, however, depend on the commitment of the individual country, which is not always guaranteed according to Camões I.P.'s staff. Involvement of partner country authorities is also not systematic for evaluations conducted by other line ministries. As for joint evaluations with other donors, Portugal has less experience – something noted already in the previous DAC peer review (OECD, 2011).

Institutional learning

Indicator: Evaluations and appropriate knowledge management systems are used as management tools

The extent to which Portugal's development co-operation system learns from its own experience is limited. Evaluation findings are not systematically used to inform decision making and there is no knowledge-sharing mechanism.

Learning from evaluations is not yet systematically part of decision making

Camões I.P. has improved its practices for learning and using evaluation findings, but it is aware that it has a long way to go to inculcate a culture of learning among all Portuguese actors involved in development co-operation. Evaluation findings are regularly shared at workshops with interested partners (CSOs, line ministries and partner country representatives). Evaluated entities are able to formally express disagreement or agreement with the findings and senior management is requested to give a final response. The Evaluation and Audit Division also publishes an annual evaluation report which highlights, among other things, progress made on implementing evaluation recommendations. The latest available annual report from the Evaluation and Audit Division states that 43% of recommendations that had been accepted were implemented, 22% were not implemented and 46% were partially implemented (Camões I.P, 2014d). This is good practice.

However, it can be difficult for Camões I.P. to follow up the degree to which recommendations are implemented as this depends on implementing agencies submitting information to Camões I.P. A lack of information from implementing agencies was flagged as an issue in the last annual evaluation report (Camões I.P. 2014e).

Portugal lacks a knowledge-sharing mechanism

Portugal's fragmented development co-operation system requires a strong knowledge management mechanism to share learning across the multitude of actors involved. No such system is currently in place. The lack of communities of practice and knowledge-sharing networks is preventing Portugal's development co-operation actors from learning fully from their experiences and improving their practice. The planned establishment of technical working groups under the Inter-ministerial Commission for Co-operation (Chapter 1) could be a step in the right direction. It would create an environment where staff from different line ministries working on the same sector can meet more systematically to discuss their experiences and challenges.

Communication, accountability and development awareness

Indicator: The member communicates development results transparently and honestly

Transparency has improved since the last peer review. Camões I.P.'s new communication strategy aims to increase the visibility of Portuguese development co-operation and foster citizens' trust. However, more regular communication with external stakeholders about the impact of all Portugal's ODA activities could enable Portugal to tell "better stories" about its work and enhance accountability. Portugal has invested strongly in development education and its work has won international acclaim.

Steps have been taken to implement the Common Standard

Portugal has improved the transparency of its development co-operation since the last peer review, as noted in Chapter 3. Committed to providing its ODA information in line with the Common Standard,[6] it now publishes forward-looking spending plans[7] and project-level data. The development of an Integrated Information System should also further enhance transparency (Box 6.1). While Portugal has published a timetable for achieving the Common Standard, it is, however, unlikely to make the December 2015 deadline of full implementation.

Box 6.1 Portugal's Integrated Information System for development co-operation

Portuguese co-operation started to develop an integrated information system in 2013-14, following its Busan commitments, to ensure conformity with the OECD-DAC regulations in terms of reporting aid. This system will have several positive impacts on the quality of Portugal's reporting:

- public and private financing institutions can input data directly through an electronic platform
- the system will be able to automatically validate data against the DAC rules
- field staff will be able to input data directly, so statistical information will better reflect the reality of Portuguese aid on the ground
- it will enable online consultation and downloads of statistical data.

Source: Camões I.P. (2015), *Memorandum of Portugal,* 16 March 2015, Government of Portugal, Lisbon.

Portugal could do more to tell stories about its development impact through social media

Complying with recommendations from the last peer review, Camões I.P. now has its own communication strategy which aims to increase the visibility of Portuguese development co-operation and to foster citizens' trust (Camões I.P. 2015a). Communication is predominately based on a digital approach.[8] Communication became more important following the merger of Portugal's former development agency and the language and culture institute. The visual identity of the former development co-operation agency became subsumed under the image of the language/culture institute. The communication department is working hard to make clear to citizens that the former language institute now also has development co-operation responsibilities.

Despite Portugal's new communication strategy, there is considerable scope for Camões I.P. to tell stories to external audiences about the impact of all of Portugal's development co-operation. Such communication would enhance the transparency, accountability and visibility of Portuguese development co-operation. Camões I.P. produces an annual report online (Camões I.P. 2014d), but it only covers its own operations (education and development) and not those of other Portuguese development actors. It could also profit from its large social media follower base to better communicate the development results of its activities or tell stories about the improvements its projects have made to people's lives in partner countries.[9] Camões I.P. should communicate more systematically on the programmes implemented by all the line ministries, so as to provide a comprehensive overview of its ODA supported activities. Accountability lines with parliament also need to be nurtured (for example, evaluations are still not presented to parliamentarians and could be a feature of parliamentary debates with some regularity, e.g. once a year).

Portugal has been praised for its good work in awareness raising for development

Portugal has its own National Strategy on Development Education 2010-2015 (IPAD 2010), which aims to integrate development and global citizenship into Portugal's formal and informal education system. Portugal's leadership in development education is the result of years of engagement with different actors from government and civil society, and dedicated funding to support development education NGOs from Camões I.P. Portugal's activities in this area have been peer reviewed and praised by different international bodies such as the Global Education Network Europe (GENE 2014) and the European Commission (EU 2012).

Notes

1 For NGOs, the obligation to submit a logical framework has been in place since 2002.

2. In June 2015, the Evaluation and Audit Division had six full-time staff. In the previous development co-operation agency – IPAD – there were only 2.5 members of staff in this division.

3. The division is now responsible for evaluation and internal audit of both development co-operation and language activities. This adds to the division's other responsibilities of quality control and risk management.

4. The 2014-16 plan indicates 15 development-related evaluations to be conducted and 5 language-related evaluations.

5. The project in question was specified as "support to infrastructure construction in Cabo Verde" and required coordination with the Ministry of Finance as responsible for the credit line which financed this project (Camões I.P. 2014c).

6. At the 4th High Level Forum on Aid Effectiveness in Busan in 2011, countries and organisations resolved to: "Implement a common, open standard for electronic publication of timely, comprehensive and forward-looking information on resources provided through development co-operation taking into account the statistical reporting of the OECD-DAC and the complementary efforts of the International Aid Transparency Initiative and others." Participants at Busan agreed to implement this standard fully by December 2015. Portugal has chosen to achieve the standard outside of the IATI process.

7. See OECD stats for the Portuguese estimates for 2014-18, https://stats.oecd.org/Index.aspx?DataSetCode=FSS/.

8. Camões I.P. uses Facebook to organise discussions and share news (the institute's Facebook profile has more than 33 000 followers). Feedback from website users has also helped Camões I.P. improve disclosure of ODA data, making them more user-friendly and machine readable.

9. A scan of Camões I.P.'s Facebook page activity during June and July 2015 shows most posts related to the culture/language activities of the institute. There was no mention of the results of projects implemented by Camões I.P. or other line ministries in partner countries. The news section of Camões I.P.'s website does link up to short documentation collecting testimonies and stories of positive development linked to Portugal's development co-operation efforts (i.e. www.instituto-camoes.pt/cooperacao/bicicletas-matutuine).

Bibliography

Government sources

Camões I.P. (2015a), *Estratégia de Comunicação*, Camões I.P. (Camões Instituto da Cooperação e da Lingua Portugal), Lisbon, Portugal, www.instituto-camoes.pt/comunicacao/estrategia-comunicacao.

Camões I.P. (2015b), *Plano de Gestão do Risco: Incluindo o Risco de Corrupção e Infrações Conexas*, Camões I.P., Lisbon, Portugal, www.instituto-camoes.pt/gestao-risco/gestao-risco.

Camões I.P. (2015c), *Memorandum of Portugal 2015*, Camões I.P., Lisbon, Portugal.

Camões I.P. (2014a), *Programa Estratégico de Cooperacão: Portugal – Timor-Leste: 2014-2017*, Camões I.P., Lisbon, Portugal, http://d3f5055r2rwsy1.cloudfront.net/images/cooperacao/pec_pt_timor1417.pdf.

Camões I.P. (2014b), *Programa de Ação de Cooperação Técnico-Policial com a República de São Tomé e Príncipe*, Camões I.P., Lisbon, Portugal.

Camões I.P. (2014c), *Plano de avaliação 2014-2016*, Government of Portugal, Lisbon.

Camões I.P. (2014d), *Relatório de actividades 2013*, Government of Portugal, Lisbon, www.instituto-camoes.pt/planos-e-relatorios-de-atividades/documentos-de-gestao/planos-e-relatorios-de-atividades/relatorio-atividades-2013-prov.

Camões I.P. (2014e), *Relatório anual da avaliação e da auditoria 2013*, Government of Portugal, Lisbon. http://d3f5055r2rwsy1.cloudfront.net/images/cooperacao/relat_avaliacao2013.pdf.

Camões I.P. (n.d.), *Cooperacão Portuguesa: Política de avaliação,* draft, Government of Portugal, Lisbon.

GOP Government of Portugal (2014), *Decreto lei 73, Diário da República* No 91, 13 May 2014, http://dre.tretas.org/dre/316970/.

IPAD (2010), Estratégia Nacional de Educação para o Desenvolvimento, *Instituto Português de Apoio ao Desenvolvimento*, Government of Portugal, Lisbon.

IPAD (n.d.), *Saúde para Todos – Programa Integrado, Instituto Português de Apoio ao Desenvolvimento*, Government of Portugal, Lisbon.

Other sources

ECDPM (2015), "Use of PCD indicators by a selection of EU member States: A brief analysis and overview", *Discussion Paper No 171, European Centre for Development Policy Management,* Maastricht http://ecdpm.org/publications/policy-coherence-indicators-eu/.

EU (2015), *Special Barometer 421: The European Year for Development, citizens' views on development, co-operation and aid*, European Union, Brussels, http://ec.europa.eu/public_opinion/archives/ebs/ebs_421_en.pdf.

EU (2012), *Commission Staff Working Document on Development Education and Awareness Raising (DEAR) in Europe*, 20 December 2012, European Commission, Brussels https://ec.europa.eu/europeaid/sites/devco/files/working-document-development-education-awareness-raising-programme-swd2012457-20121220_en.pdf.

OECD (2011), *OECD Development Assistance Peer Reviews: Portugal 2010,* OECD Publishing, Paris. http://dx.doi.org/10.1787/9789264098312-en.

OECD (2010), *Quality Standards for Development Evaluation*, Development Assistance Committee, OECD, Paris, www.oecd.org/development/evaluation/qualitystandards.pdf.

Chapter 7: Portugal's humanitarian assistance

Strategic framework

Indicator: Clear political directives and strategies for resilience, response and recovery

Portugal could consider how to use its domestic crisis preparedness skills to more systematically build the capacity of civil protection services in partner countries – this might be a useful focus area for the new strategic framework for the humanitarian programme. Setting out such a framework would also allow Portugal to advocate for a dedicated humanitarian budget line, and thus increase its overall humanitarian volume, in line with international burden-sharing agreements.

Humanitarian assistance has a brand new strategic framework

The 2010 peer review recommended that Portugal set out a strategic framework for its humanitarian assistance (OECD, 2010); a new Operational Strategy had just been finalised as the peer review was completed (Portugal, 2015), after several attempts (Box 1). It will be interesting to see how this new Operational Strategy changes Portugal's approach to humanitarian programming.

Box 7.1 Key features of Portugal's new Operational Action Strategy for Humanitarian Action

Portugal's new strategy was approved on 27 August 2015. It includes the following features:

- reference to the Good Humanitarian Donorship principles and to other internationally recognised humanitarian instruments
- application of international guidelines on the use of military and civil defence assets
- a commitment to build resilience and reduce risks, including through regular Strategic Cooperation Programmes (development programmes)
- allows for funding of rehabilitation and resilience activities
- a clear statement that Camoes I.P. will co-ordinate cross-government humanitarian efforts
- promotion of a balance between bilateral and multilateral responses, and of a special financing facility for NGOs involved in humanitarian assistance
- intentions to promote training and build human resource competence on humanitarian assistance.

Source: Portugal (2015*), Estratégia Operacional de Ação Humanitária e de Emergência, Diário da República,* 1.ª série — N.º 167 — 27 August 2015.

Development and humanitarian responses are not joined up

Portugal does not yet have a holistic development and humanitarian response, and Portugal's country strategies (Indicative Cooperation Programmes/Strategic Cooperation Programmes) do not include humanitarian issues or consider how to minimise the risks of crises and shocks. This is despite the potential of these shocks to undermine development investments and hinder progress towards sustainable development. The new Operational Strategy does, however, outline plans for greater coherence between these two instruments, including plans to include disaster risk reduction considerations in future Strategic Cooperation Programmes.

More systematic use of civil protection to build capacity in partner countries could be useful

Portugal could consider how to help partner governments minimise the risks of disaster, and thus diminish the potential impact of crises and shocks on their institutions, infrastructure and citizens. The Civil Protection Mechanism, under the Ministry of Interior, has proven itself capable during domestic crises; it also supports disaster response in partner countries. Leveraging these skills to partner country civil defence systems could be a useful way to boost their capacity to reduce risk. The Ministry of Health has also demonstrated competence in this area, for example supporting Ebola preparedness in Guinea by providing medical laboratories. Volcanologists have also been sent to Cabo Verde to help monitor the Fogo volcano. Some disaster preparedness projects – particularly for NGOs working in the water sector – have also received Portuguese funding, often co-financed by the European Commission.

Portugal is the smallest humanitarian DAC donor

There is no budget line for humanitarian assistance in Portugal. All funding allocations are made either by the Ministry of Finance from additional funds for specific crises, or from undisbursed funds originally allocated to development programmes. Some supplementary funding is available from the budgets of the ministries of health and defence, but this is difficult to access. Between 2010 and 2013 Portugal disbursed just USD 1.065 million in humanitarian assistance, plus some small grants to the Central Emergency Response Fund, making it the smallest OECD/DAC humanitarian donor.[1]

Effective programme design

Indicator: Programmes target the highest risk to life and livelihood

Decisions on where, and how, to respond to crises are often made on an ad hoc basis at the political level. This risks generating misconceptions about Portugal's respect for key humanitarian principles such as independence and impartiality. Portugal is careful, however, to align its bilateral responses with requests from partner countries. Drawing up funding guidelines could help further mitigate this risk.

Decision making appears ad hoc and political

The 2010 peer review noted that Portugal tends to use its humanitarian funding for small-scale responses to sudden onset crises; this remains largely the case. Decisions are often made at a political level as crises arise. Portugal will need to take care to demonstrate that it respects fundamental humanitarian principles, especially independence and impartiality,[2] in deciding where and how to respond. Publicly available funding guidelines would be a good first step to support this type of principled decision making.

No clear link between early warnings

As with many DAC members, there is no clear link between early warnings of humanitarian crises, and early Portuguese response to mitigate the effects of these crises.

Responses linked to partner country requests

The participation of affected communities in Portugal's humanitarian responses is not actively promoted. However, Portugal's civil protection responses do all follow formal requests made by partner countries.

Effective delivery, partnerships and instruments

Indicator: Delivery modalities and partnerships help deliver quality programmes

Despite a lack of funds for humanitarian partners, Portugal continues to offer support where it can. Most of the humanitarian programme is implemented through bilateral responses via the civil protection service, often co-funded by the European Union, and through contributions to the global pooled funding mechanism. There are good relationships with partner country governments who request relief goods in times of crisis. Funding to other humanitarian partners is unpredictable and last minute; this may change under the new strategic framework document.

Portugal manages to support protracted crises despite budget cuts

Portugal notes that it has allocated humanitarian funds to four UN agencies and to the Red Cross movement in the past (GOP, 2015); but budgetary restrictions since 2011 have meant that these contributions have dried up in recent years. Portugal is to be given credit for continuing to support other initiatives, however. A good example is its support to the UN's Refugee Agency's (UNHCR) Confidence Building Measures, which aim to address the effects of prolonged separation of Saharan refugees in camps near Tindouf, Algeria from their families in Western Sahara through cultural seminars, a programme of family visits and co-ordination meetings.[3]

Portugal's rapid response operates through civil protection and the CERF

Responses to sudden onset emergencies are the backbone of Portugal's current humanitarian programme. On a global scale, Portugal makes regular contributions from undisbursed development funds to the global Central Emergency Response Fund's (CERF) pooled fund. However, the size of the allocations has decreased significantly since 2012.[4] Requests for civil defence responses – including the response to the 2014 eruption of the Pico do Fogo volcano in Cabo Verde – are routed through the Ministry of Foreign Affairs to the Ministry of the Interior, which endeavours to send relief items that match the request made by the affected country. The peer review team has verified this by reviewing the official request sent by Cabo Verde to the EU Civil Protection Mechanism and ensuring that the goods dispatched matched those on the request.[5] The transport costs for these bilateral responses are often co-financed (55%) by the EU Civil Protection Mechanism.[6]

Funding for humanitarian partners is slow and unpredictable

Portugal's humanitarian partners have no predictability over funding allocations; timeliness is also an issue. The lack of a budget line has meant that any funding is provided at the last minute, once undisbursed funds from development programmes have been gathered together. Partners have also found it difficult to engage on policy issues in the absence of a strategic framework setting out Portugal's objectives and funding criteria; this may change with the new Operational Action Strategy. However, relationships with partner governments are strong, and this helps ensure that bilateral responses – mostly in-kind aid – are appropriate.

Portugal is active in EU donor co-ordination mechanisms

Portugal is an active participant of the European humanitarian co-ordination mechanism, the Committee on Humanitarian Aid and Food Aid (COHAFA).

Organisation fit for purpose

Indicator: Systems, structures, processes and people work together effectively and efficiently

Bilateral response operations – mostly in-kind aid – are ably co-ordinated by the Ministry of Interior, building on its domestic co-ordination role. Portugal now needs to look for a mechanism to link these responses to development co-ordination programmes and to the wider international response system. Military assets are often used to deliver relief goods and provide technical support; Portugal will need to apply its new guidelines for its involvement to demonstrate compliance with international agreements.

Co-ordination across government is limited to bilateral responses

The 2010 peer review recommended that Portugal formalise a cross-government humanitarian co-ordination body and conduct regular simulation exercises (OECD, 2010). During the response to the 2005 Indian Ocean tsunami, Portugal set up a National Operations Co-ordination Centre. Although this proved an effective mechanism for co-ordination, it has not been used since. While Camões I.P. has the co-ordination mandate for international responses, in practice Portugal follows its domestic model, with operations co-ordinated through the Ministry of Interior, the home of the Civil Protection Mechanism. This model functions well for bilateral response operations, but Portugal still lacks a way to systematically link its bilateral responses to development programmes and to international response efforts. A mechanism for this type of cross-government co-ordination has been included in the new Operational Action Plan.

Portugal needs to reinforce its approach to civil-military co-ordination

Portugal has no civil-military policy or standard procedures. This is a risk given the regular use of the military to deliver relief goods and provide technical support for humanitarian responses. There are international agreements that cover the deployment of military and civil defence assets in disaster relief (IASC, 2008; OCHA, 2007); Portugal has now included reference to these in the Operational Action Plan. This will hopefully provide clarity over the principled use of military assets: for example, in Portugal's response to the Pico do Fogo volcanic eruption it is unclear 1) how it ensured that the use of military personnel was necessary because of a lack of civilian alternatives, 2) that the use of military assets was based on a clear cost-benefit analysis, and 3) the steps it took to ensure that the operations were of a civilian nature.

No dedicated humanitarian staff

The 2010 peer review recommended that adequate staff should be allocated to implement the humanitarian programme; however, this has not been possible in the general climate of government staff cut-backs (Chapter 4).

Results, learning and accountability

Indicator: Results are measured and communicated, and lessons learnt

Results and learning are not a priority for the humanitarian programme, given its size. However, the Civil Protection Mechanism does seek to improve its work by learning from international deployments; this is good practice. Better communication of the results of Portugal's humanitarian assistance could help build political consensus around the need for a bigger and broader humanitarian programme.

Bilateral responses are reviewed	The Civil Protection Mechanism and the Ministry of Health review their international deployments to support better quality responses in the future; this is good practice.
Portugal relies on third party evaluations	Funding to UN partners is not monitored; instead Portugal relies on external evaluation processes, such as the regular evaluations of the CERF programme.[7] This is appropriate given the size of the funds allocated.
Lack of results dissemination is a missed opportunity	The results of the humanitarian programme are not disseminated externally. This misses an opportunity to increase the political will for a more extensive humanitarian programme.

Notes

1. Source: OECD Creditor Reporting System. Figures in USD Constant Prices, Gross Disbursements.

2. Impartiality: humanitarian action must be carried out on the basis of need alone, giving priority to the most urgent cases of distress and making no distinctions on the basis of nationality, race, gender, religious belief, class or political opinions. Independence: humanitarian action must be autonomous from the political, economic, military or other objectives that any actor may hold with regard to areas where humanitarian action is being implemented. More on humanitarian principles at https://docs.unocha.org/sites/dms/Documents/OOM-humanitarianprinciples_eng_June12.pdf.

3. More on the Confidence Building Measures programme at www.unhcr.org/532708166.html.

4. Up until 2012, Portugal was providing EUR 200 000 a year (around USD 267 000) to the Central Emergency Response Fund. Since then, it has provided EUR 50 000 (around USD 61 000) a year. See www.unocha.org/cerf/our-donors/funding/cerf-pledges-and-contributions-2006-2015.

5. For a summary, refer to the ECHO *Civil Protection Messages* (ECHO, 2014a and 2014b).

6. For more on the EU Civil Protection Mechanism, see http://ec.europa.eu/echo/what/civil-protection/mechanism_en.

7. External evaluations of the CERF can be found at www.unocha.org/cerf/reportsevaluations/evaluations-and-studies.

Bibliography

Government sources

Camões I.P. (2015c), *Memorandum of Portugal 2015*, Camões I.P., Lisbon, Portugal.

Portugal (2015), *Estratégia Operacional de Ação Humanitária e de Emergência*, Diário da República, 1.ª série — N.º 167 — 27 de agosto de 2015

Other sources

GHD (2003), *The Principles and Good Practice of Humanitarian Donorship,* declaration signed in Stockholm, 2003, http://www.ifrc.org/Docs/idrl/I267EN.pdf.

ECHO (2014a), *Cabo Verde Volcanic Eruption: ECHO Civil Protection Message N°1,* Internal European Commission document, European Commission Humanitarian Aid and Civil Protection, Brussels.

ECHO (2014b), *Cabo Verde Volcanic Eruption: ECHO Civil Protection Message N°2,* Internal European Commission document, European Commission Humanitarian Aid and Civil Protection, Brussels.

EU (2007), "Joint Statement by the Council and the Representatives of the Governments of the Member States meeting within the Council, the European Parliament and the European Commission – The European Consensus on Humanitarian Aid", Official Journal C 25 of 30.1.2008, European Union, Brussels.

IASC (2008), *Civil-Military Guidelines and Reference for Complex Emergencies (2008), comprising: – Guidelines on the Use of Military and Civil Defence Assets to Support United Nations Humanitarian Activities in Complex Emergencies – "MCDA Guidelines" Rev. 1 (January 2006), Civil-Military Relationship in Complex Emergencies – an IASC Reference Paper (June 2004) and Use of Military or Armed Escorts for Humanitarian Convoys – IASC Discussion Paper and Non-Binding Guidelines (September 2001),* Inter Agency Steering Committee, with the United Nations Office for the Co-ordination of Humanitarian Affairs, Geneva.

OCHA (2007), *Guidelines on the Use of Foreign Military and Civil Defence Assets in Disaster Relief – "Oslo Guidelines" - Rev. 1.1,* United Nations Office for the Co-ordination of Humanitarian Affairs, Geneva.

OECD (2011), *OECD Development Assistance Peer Reviews: Portugal 2010,* OECD Publishing, Paris. http://dx.doi.org/10.1787/9789264098312-en.

Annex A: Progress since the 2010 DAC peer review recommendations

Key Issues: Development beyond aid

Recommendations 2010	Progress in implementation
Apply the new law on policy coherence for development, including by:	
I. strengthening the institutions or co-ordination mechanisms with a mandate, tools and authority to promote PCD	**Implemented**
II. establishing systems to monitor, analyse and report on the development impacts of Portugal's policies on partner countries.	**Partially implemented**
Revisit its approach to engaging the private sector in development: Specifically, it should give IPAD a full seat on the SOFID board and, over the next three years, evaluate the extent to which SOFID has contributed to development and poverty reduction in partner countries.	**Partially implemented**

Key Issues: Strategic orientations

Recommendations 2010	Progress in implementation
Use the planned update of its *Strategic Vision* as an opportunity to: I. set out how it will reduce the fragmentation of its programmes and make use of different aid modalities II. plan how to improve mainstreaming of gender equality and environment III. encourage engagement with and support from civil society and parliamentarians IV. Reiterate that language instruction, when funded by ODA, should only be used to promote development.	**Partially Implemented**

Key Issues: Aid volume, channels and allocations

Recommendations 2010	Progress in implementation
Establish realistic interim targets for significant increases in ODA by 2015, embed these multi-year binding targets in the state budget and stick to them. It should also work within the EU framework to meet its commitment to achieve the 0.7% target. As the economic situation improves, the DAC expects that Portugal will speed up its efforts to meet its international commitments.	**Recommendation not met**
Continue to increase its sectorial focus while also reducing the large number of standalone small projects and investing in larger projects or programmes.	**Partially implemented**
Increasingly complement its use of technical co-operation with grant modalities which involve greater financial transfers to partner countries particularly as it scales up Portuguese ODA.	**Recommendation not met**
Ensure that lines of credit are used with caution in order to: I. protect the focus of the development program and II. comply with the DAC Recommendation on the Terms and Conditions of Aid.	**Recommendation not met**

Key Issues: Organisation and management

Recommendations 2010	Progress in implementation
Review its overall business model to reduce the fragmentation of the system and the budget and to further improve co-ordination, oversight, efficiency, effectiveness and accountability. Over the long term it should increase consolidation of the ODA budget within the institution responsible for overall co-ordination of development co-operation.	**Partially implemented**
Agree in writing, that IPAD should be involved right from the early stages of line ministries' project formulation, not just at the project approval stage.	**Implemented**

Agree strategic partnerships with municipalities in order to align development co-operation priorities and activities.	**Implemented**
Reform the human resources framework to enable greater staff mobility and the recruitment and retention of specialists. In its six main partner countries it should also delegate more authority and ensure the right type of skills to increase capacity in its embassies.	**Partially implemented**

Key Issues: Delivery and partnerships

Recommendations 2010	Progress in implementation
Ensure that the next generation of country strategies explicitly commit Portugal to: I. use partner country systems II. make use of programme-based approaches and ensure small projects are situated within or closely linked to larger programmes III. increase co-ordination with other donors.	**Implemented**
Increase the predictability and transparency of its aid by securing multi-year figures in its state budget, and by providing regular information on aid commitments and disbursements to all partner countries, so that they can be reflected in their budgets.	**Implemented**
Build strategic partnerships with some key domestic and partner country NGOs, for example by introducing multi-year strategic framework agreements.	**Partially implemented**
Continue to untie more of its ODA and protect the progress it has already made in untying by reviewing the tying terms of its existing lines of credit and ensuring that any future lines offer untied loans only. It should also ensure that the tying status of both its grants and loans is properly reported.	**Recommendation not met**

Turn its commitment to capacity development (CD) into practice by: I. co-ordinating more of its technical co-operation II. reducing the dominance of expatriate expertise in favour of local or South-South exchanges III. identifying incentives for line ministries to focus on building capacity with a view to phasing out their involvement IV. requiring all ODA-eligible activities to identify how they will contribute to capacity.	**Not Examined**

Key Issues: Results management and accountability

Recommendations 2010	Progress in implementation
Develop a communications strategy which sets out how Portugal will pro-actively engage key target groups (other parts of government parliamentarians and media), demonstrate development results and build a wider base of public support for Portuguese development co-operation.	**Partially implemented**

Key Issues: Humanitarian assistance

Recommendations 2010	Progress in implementation
Develop an overarching policy and funding guidelines for humanitarian action that embody the GHD principles and focus on areas where Portugal could clearly add value, such as disaster response and preparedness. Adequate humanitarian action staff should be allocated to develop and implement this policy.	**Recommendation not met**
Formalise an inclusive cross-ministry Portuguese humanitarian co-ordination body and conduct regular humanitarian emergency simulation exercises.	**Recommendation not met**

Figure A.1 Portugal's implementation of 2010 peer review recommendations

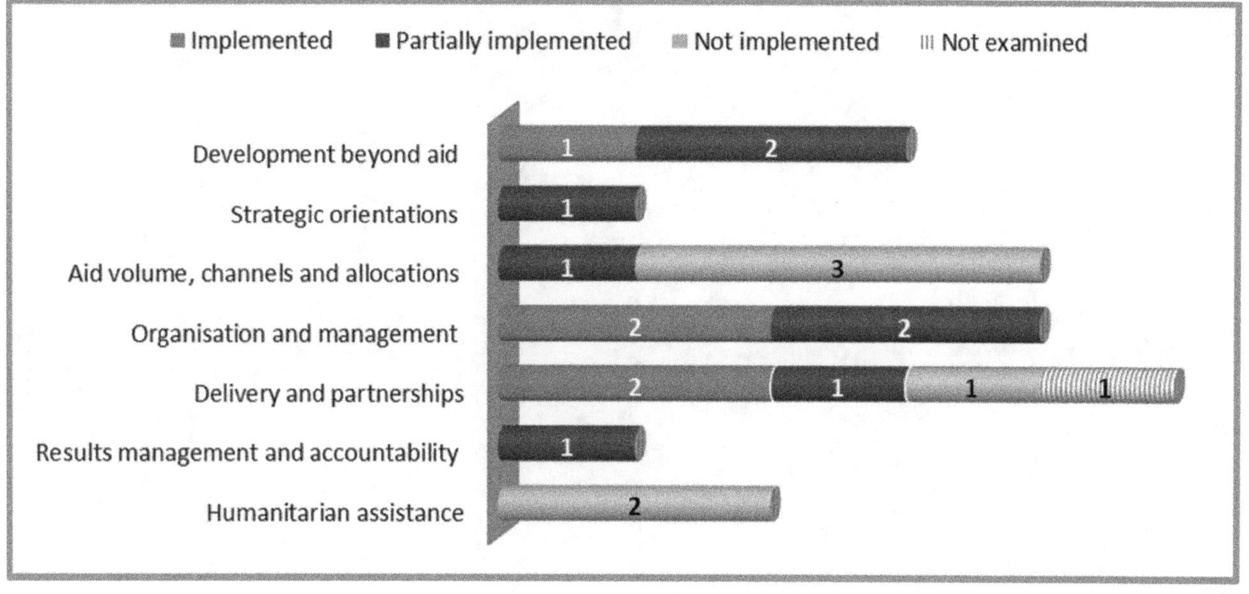

Annex B: OECD/DAC standard suite of tables

Table B.1 Total financial flows

USD million at current prices and exchange rates

Portugal	1999-2003	2004-2008	2009	2010	2011	2012	2013
					Net disbursements		
Total official flows	**328**	**389**	**513**	**649**	**708**	**583**	**491**
Official development assistance	**291**	**579**	**513**	**649**	**708**	**581**	**488**
Bilateral	188	389	277	396	477	397	303
Multilateral	104	190	236	253	231	184	186
Other official flows	**36**	**- 191**	**-**	**-**	**1**	**2**	**3**
Bilateral	36	- 191	-	-	1	2	3
Multilateral	-	-	-	-	-	-	-
Net Private Grants	**2**	**3**	**4**	**5**	**5**	**7**	**7**
Private flows at market terms	**1 705**	**847**	**-1 577**	**- 492**	**-2 013**	**- 114**	**1 776**
Bilateral: *of which*	1 705	847	-1 577	- 492	-2 013	- 114	1 776
Direct investment	1 475	535	-2 271	-1 225	- 705	- 366	- 706
Export credits	230	331	757	919	84	- 36	155
Multilateral	-	-	-	-	-	-	-
Total flows	**2 035**	**1 239**	**-1 060**	**162**	**-1 299**	**475**	**2 275**
for reference:							
ODA (at constant 2013 USD million)	*499*	*650*	*500*	*661*	*689*	*614*	*488*
ODA (as a % of GNI)	*0.25*	*0.30*	*0.23*	*0.29*	*0.31*	*0.28*	*0.23*
Total flows (as a % of GNI) (a)	*1.75*	*0.64*	*-0.48*	*0.07*	*-0.57*	*0.23*	*1.06*
ODA to and channelled through NGOs							
- In USD million	2	9	8	23	21	16	15
- In percentage of total net ODA	1	2	2	3	3	3	3
- DAC countries' average % of total net ODA	*8*	*8*	*7*	*8*	*9*	*13*	*13*

a. To countries eligible for ODA.

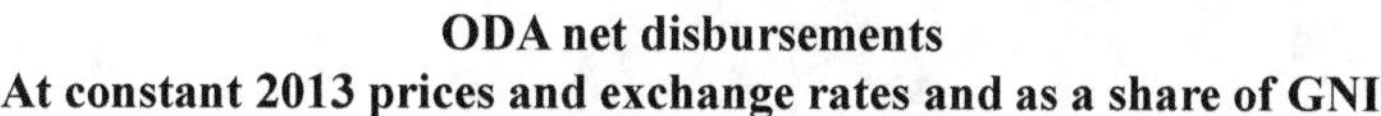

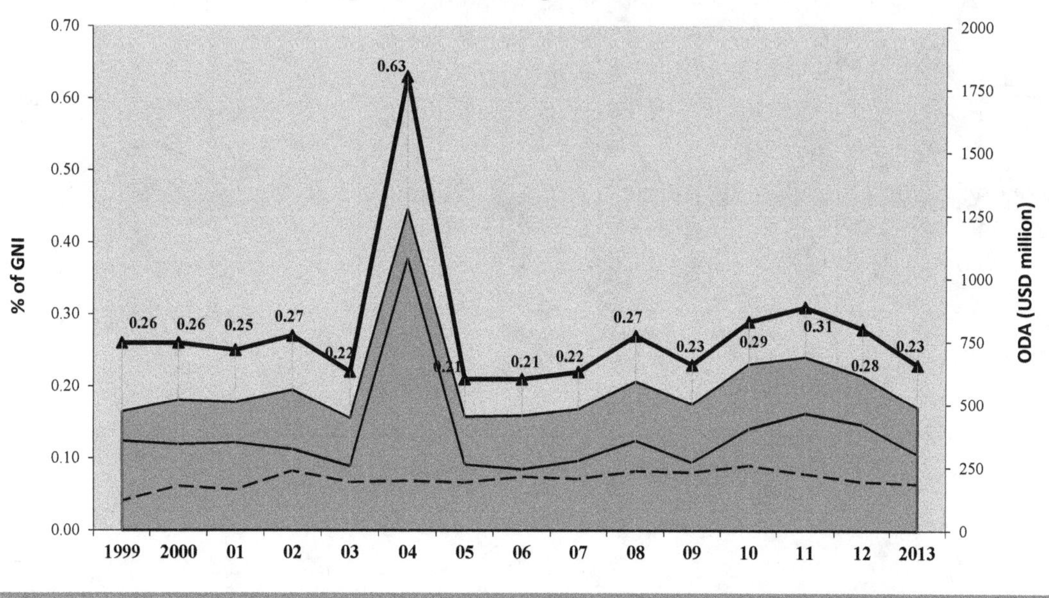

Table B.2 ODA by main categories

Disbursements

Portugal	Constant 2013 USD million					Per cent share of gross disbursements					Total DAC 2013%
	2009	2010	2011	2012	2013	2009	2010	2011	2012	2013	
Gross Bilateral ODA	**305**	**440**	**501**	**460**	**343**	**57**	**63**	**69**	**70**	**65**	**73**
Budget support	-	5	5	4	3	-	1	1	1	1	4
of which: General budget support	3	5	5	4	3	1	1	1	1	1	2
Core contributions & pooled prog.& funds	-	2	3	0	0	-	0	0	0	0	13
of which: Core support to national NGOs	0	0	0	0	0	0	0	0	0	0	1
Core support to international NGOs	0	0	0	-	-	0	0	0	-	-	1
Core support to PPPs	-	0	0	-	-	-	0	0	-	-	0
Project-type interventions	-	294	418	398	290	-	42	58	61	55	38
of which: Investment projects	96	223	346	326	217	18	32	48	50	41	12
Experts and other technical assistance	-	71	28	9	3	-	10	4	1	1	4
Scholarships and student costs in donor countries	-	40	26	28	23	-	6	4	4	4	2
of which: Imputed student costs	36	27	14	13	13	7	4	2	2	3	1
Debt relief grants	2	4	5	7	9	0	1	1	1	2	4
Administrative costs	18	21	14	12	12	3	3	2	2	2	4
Other in-donor expenditures	3	3	2	2	2	1	0	0	0	0	3
of which: refugees in donor countries	0	0	0	1	2						
Gross Multilateral ODA	**230**	**258**	**224**	**194**	**186**	**43**	**37**	**31**	**30**	**35**	**27**
UN agencies	13	14	10	12	17	2	2	1	2	3	5
EU institutions	184	188	176	163	157	34	27	24	25	30	8
World Bank group	3	22	20	2	2	0	3	3	0	0	6
Regional development banks	24	29	14	15	8	4	4	2	2	1	3
Other multilateral	7	5	5	3	2	1	1	1	0	0	6
Total gross ODA	**535**	**697**	**726**	**654**	**528**	**100**	**100**	**100**	**100**	**100**	**100**
Repayments and debt cancellation	**- 35**	**- 36**	**- 37**	**- 40**	**- 40**						
Total net ODA	**500**	**661**	**689**	**614**	**488**						
For reference:											
Free standing technical co-operation	*141*	*99*	*96*	*80*	*70*						
Net debt relief	*0*	*0*	*0*	-	-						

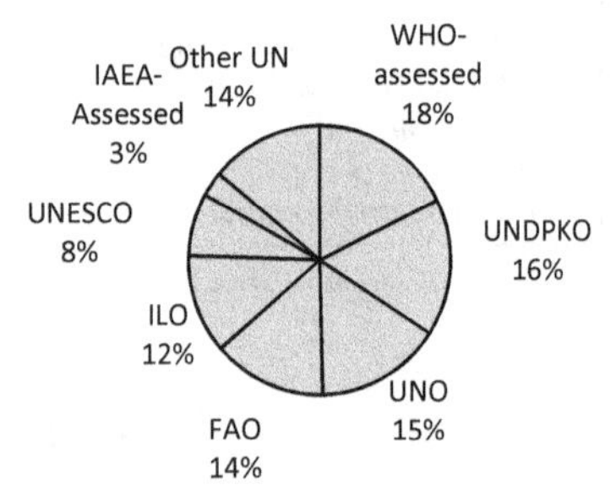

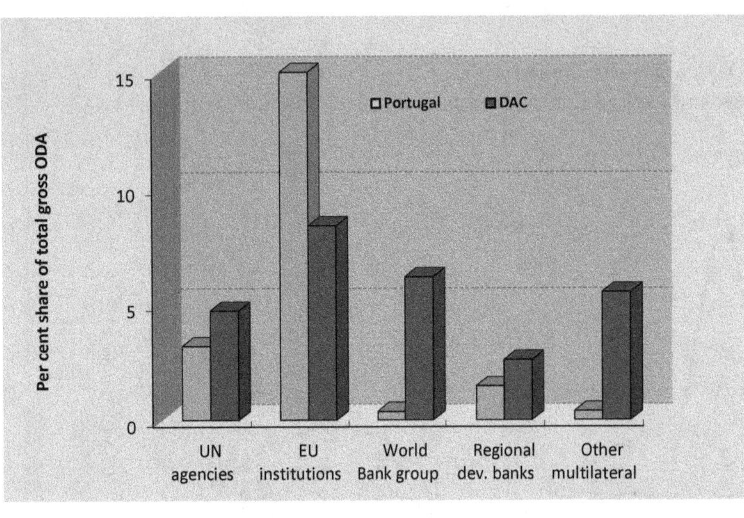

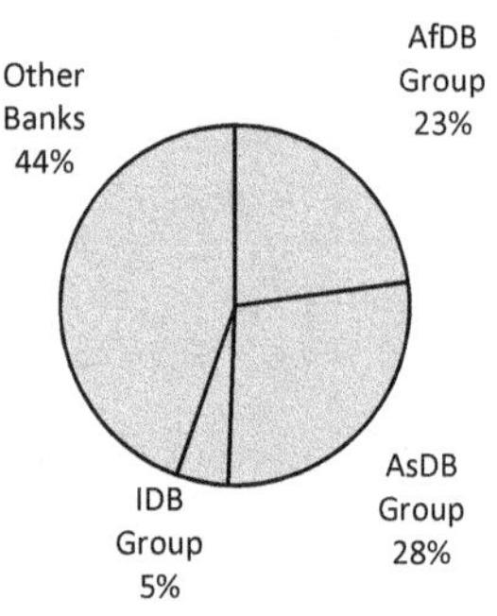

Table B.3 Bilateral ODA allocable by region and income group

Gross disbursements

Portugal	Constant 2013 USD million					Per cent share					Total DAC
	2009	2010	2011	2012	2013	2009	2010	2011	2012	2013	2013%
Africa	202	331	434	403	286	72	81	90	90	88	40
Sub-Saharan Africa	182	330	433	341	286	65	81	90	76	88	34
North Africa	20	0	0	62	0	7	0	0	14	0	4
Asia	46	50	36	34	31	17	12	7	8	10	37
South and Central Asia	12	15	3	3	1	4	4	1	1	0	24
Far East	34	34	33	31	30	12	8	7	7	9	12
America	3	10	10	9	7	1	2	2	2	2	9
North and Central America	0	0	1	0	0	0	0	0	0	0	4
South America	2	9	9	7	5	1	2	2	2	2	4
Middle East	10	0	0	0	0	4	0	0	0	0	9
Oceania	0	-	-	-	-	0	-	-	-	-	2
Europe	18	17	2	0	2	6	4	0	0	0	3
Total bilateral allocable by region	**280**	**408**	**481**	**446**	**326**	**100**	**100**	**100**	**100**	**100**	**100**
Least developed	162	226	310	180	139	60	56	65	41	43	44
Other low-income	0	0	0	0	0	0	0	0	0	0	4
Lower middle-income	90	150	150	244	164	33	37	32	55	51	34
Upper middle-income	18	25	15	18	20	7	6	3	4	6	18
More advanced developing countries	0	0	-	-	-	0	0	-	-	-	0
Total bilateral allocable by income	**271**	**402**	**475**	**442**	**323**	**100**	**100**	**100**	**100**	**100**	**100**
For reference:											
Total bilateral	305	440	501	460	343	*100*	*100*	*100*	*100*	*100*	*100*
of which: Unallocated by region	*24*	*32*	*20*	*14*	*16*	*8*	*7*	*4*	*3*	*5*	*25*
of which: Unallocated by income	*34*	*37*	*26*	*18*	*20*	*11*	*8*	*5*	*4*	*6*	*31*

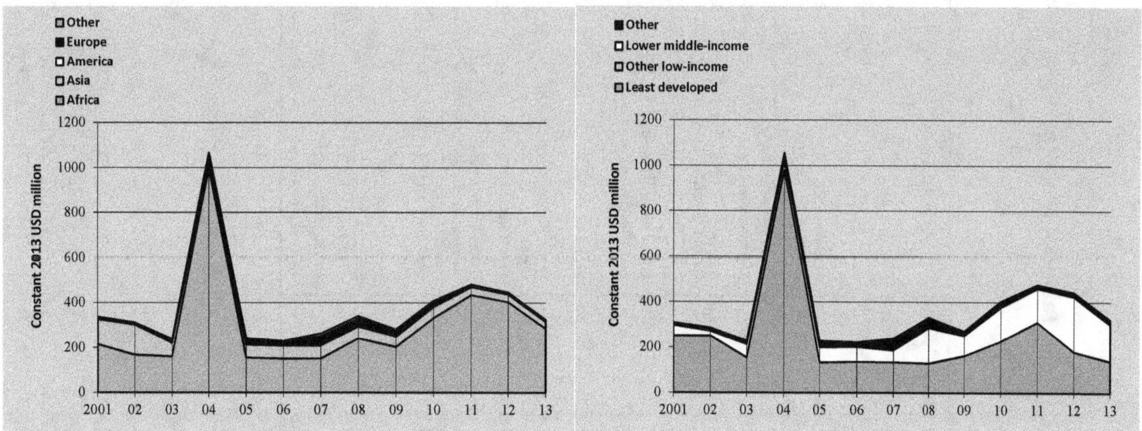

1. Each region includes regional amounts which cannot be allocated by sub-region. The sum of the sub-regional amounts may therefore fall short of the regional total.

Table B.4 Main recipients of bilateral ODA

Gross disbursements

Portugal	2002-06 average Current USD million	Constant 2013 USD mln	Per cent share	Memo: DAC countries' average %
Angola	158	197	47	
Timor-Leste	43	61	13	
Cabo Verde	39	49	11	
Mozambique	22	30	7	
Sao Tome and Principe	12	16	4	
Top 5 recipients	**274**	**353**	**81**	**50**
Guinea-Bissau	11	14	3	
Iraq	5	7	2	
Bosnia and Herzegovina	5	6	2	
Afghanistan	3	4	1	
Serbia	3	3	1	
Top 10 recipients	**302**	**388**	**89**	**68**
Democratic Republic of the Congo	2	3	1	
Sierra Leone	2	2	0	
Brazil	1	1	0	
Indonesia	1	1	0	
South Africa	1	1	0	
Top 15 recipients	**308**	**396**	**91**	**76**
States Ex-Yugoslavia	1	1	0	
Ethiopia	1	1	0	
Rwanda	1	1	0	
Sudan	0	1	0	
West Bank and Gaza Strip	0	1	0	
Top 20 recipients	**311**	**400**	**92**	**80**
Total (74 recipients)	**315**	**405**	**93**	
Unallocated	23	31	7	5
Total bilateral gross	**338**	**435**	**100**	**100**

	2007-11 average Current USD million	Constant 2013 USD mln	Per cent share	Memo: DAC countries' average %
Cabo Verde	95	94	25	
Mozambique	91	90	24	
Timor-Leste	36	36	9	
Morocco	23	22	6	
Sao Tome and Principe	19	19	5	
Top 5 recipients	**266**	**262**	**69**	**37**
Angola	18	18	5	
Guinea-Bissau	15	15	4	
Afghanistan	10	10	3	
Serbia	9	9	2	
Bosnia and Herzegovina	9	9	2	
Top 10 recipients	**328**	**323**	**85**	**51**
Lebanon	6	6	2	
Brazil	5	5	1	
Kosovo	2	2	1	
China (People's Republic of)	1	1	0	
Chad	1	1	0	
Top 15 recipients	**344**	**339**	**90**	**55**
States Ex-Yugoslavia	1	1	0	
Democratic Republic of the Cor	1	1	0	
Rwanda	1	1	0	
West Bank and Gaza Strip	1	1	0	
India	0	0	0	
Top 20 recipients	**347**	**342**	**90**	**58**
Total (77 recipients)	**350**	**345**	**91**	
Unallocated	33	33	9	24
Total bilateral gross	**383**	**378**	**100**	**100**

	2012-13 average Current USD million	Constant 2013 USD mln	Per cent share	Memo: DAC countries average %
Cabo Verde	166	171	43	
Mozambique	82	84	21	
Morocco	29	31	8	
Angola	24	25	6	
Sao Tome and Principe	19	20	5	
Top 5 recipients	**320**	**331**	**82**	**36**
Timor-Leste	19	19	5	
China (People's Republic of)	11	11	3	
Guinea-Bissau	9	9	2	
Brazil	6	6	1	
Afghanistan	1	1	0	
Top 10 recipients	**365**	**377**	**94**	**50**
South Africa	1	1	0	
States Ex-Yugoslavia	1	1	0	
Rwanda	0	0	0	
India	0	0	0	
Senegal	0	0	0	
Top 15 recipients	**368**	**380**	**95**	**57**
Syrian Arab Republic	0	0	0	
Namibia	0	0	0	
Indonesia	0	0	0	
Guinea	0	0	0	
Kosovo	0	0	0	
Top 20 recipients	**369**	**381**	**95**	**61**
Total (82 recipients)	**371**	**383**	**95**	
Unallocated	18	19	5	28
Total bilateral gross	**389**	**401**	**100**	**100**

Table B.5 Bilateral ODA by major purposes at constant prices and exchange rates

Commitments - Two-year average

Portugal	2002-2006 average		2007-11 average		2012-13 average		2012-13
	2013 USD million	Per cent	2013 USD million	Per cent	2013 USD million	Per cent	Total DAC per cent
Social infrastructure & services	**178**	**41**	**170**	**46**	**136**	**37**	**39**
Education	74	17	70	19	54	15	8
of which: basic education	6	1	3	1	0	0	2
Health	12	3	11	3	16	4	6
of which: basic health	1	0	2	1	2	0	4
Population & reproductive health	0	0	1	0	1	0	7
Water supply & sanitation	1	0	1	0	0	0	5
Government & civil society	62	14	66	18	13	3	12
of which: Conflict, peace & security	16	4	52	14	7	2	2
Other social infrastructure & services	28	7	23	6	53	14	2
Economic infrastructure & services	**19**	**5**	**49**	**13**	**22**	**6**	**18**
Transport & storage	14	3	32	9	0	0	8
Communications	2	1	2	1	1	0	0
Energy	1	0	14	4	20	5	6
Banking & financial services	1	0	1	0	1	0	2
Business & other services	1	0	0	0	0	0	1
Production sectors	**7**	**2**	**3**	**1**	**1**	**0**	**7**
Agriculture, forestry & fishing	4	1	3	1	1	0	5
Industry, mining & construction	2	1	0	0	0	0	1
Trade & tourism	1	0	0	0	0	0	1
Multisector	**16**	**4**	**11**	**3**	**5**	**1**	**9**
Commodity and programme aid	**4**	**1**	**120**	**32**	**194**	**52**	**4**
Action relating to debt	**181**	**42**	**2**	**1**	**-**	**-**	**3**
Humanitarian aid	**10**	**2**	**1**	**0**	**0**	**0**	**9**
Administrative costs of donors	**14**	**3**	**16**	**4**	**12**	**3**	**6**
Refugees in donor countries	**0**	**0**	**0**	**0**	**1**	**0**	**4**
Total bilateral allocable	**428**	**100**	**373**	**100**	**370**	**100**	**100**
For reference:							
Total bilateral	*435*	*68*	*378*	*63*	*371*	*61*	*74*
of which: Unallocated	*7*	*1*	*5*	*1*	*1*	*0*	*1*
Total multilateral	*205*	*32*	*225*	*37*	*238*	*39*	*26*
Total ODA	***640***	***100***	***603***	***100***	***609***	***100***	***100***

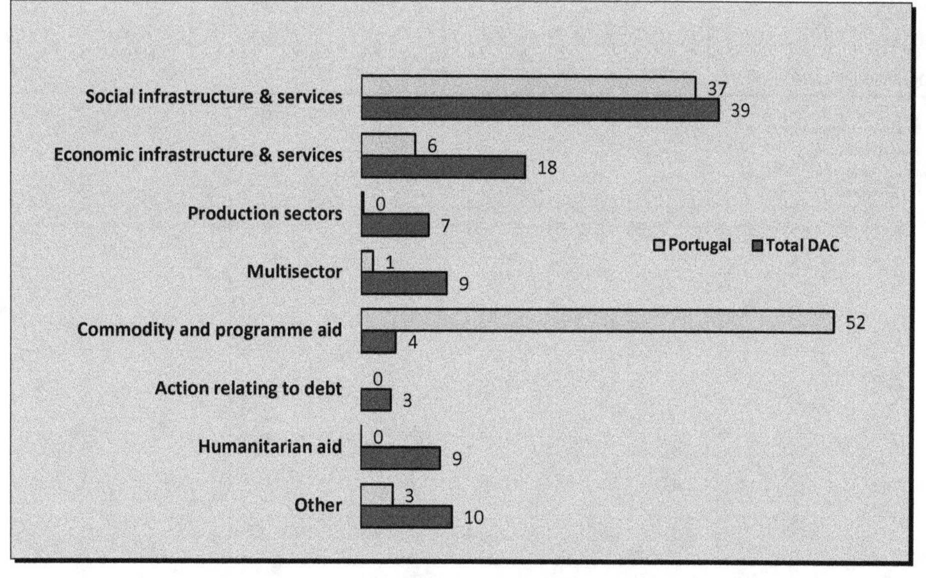

Table B.6 Comparative aid performance

Table 6. Comparative aid performance

Net disbursements

	Official development assistance			Grant element of ODA (commitments) 2013	Share of multilateral aid 2013				ODA to LDCs Bilateral and through multilateral agencies 2013	
	2013		2007-08 to 2012-13 Average annual % change in real terms		% of ODA		% of GNI			
	USD million	% of GNI		% (a)	(b)	(c)	(b)	(c)	% of ODA	% of GNI
Australia	4 846	0.33	5.8	99.9	14.0		0.05		26.8	0.09
Austria	1 171	0.27	-8.5	100.0	53.6	28.1	0.15	0.08	29.1	0.08
Belgium	2 300	0.45	1.0	99.8	43.2	21.6	0.20	0.10	35.3	0.16
Canada	4 947	0.27	0.8	100.0	29.0		0.08		37.3	0.10
Czech Republic	211	0.11	0.3	100.0	73.0	16.9	0.08	0.02	24.7	0.03
Denmark	2 927	0.85	0.5	100.0	26.8	17.9	0.23	0.15	31.6	0.27
Finland	1 435	0.54	4.6	100.0	42.7	28.9	0.23	0.15	35.4	0.19
France	11 339	0.41	2.9	84.4	40.0	20.0	0.16	0.08	28.6	0.12
Germany	14 228	0.38	0.8	86.9	33.6	15.2	0.13	0.06	23.6	0.09
Greece	239	0.10	-13.5	100.0	81.8	6.5	0.08	0.01	18.7	0.02
Iceland	35	0.25	-4.7	100.0	15.8		0.04		46.0	0.12
Ireland	846	0.46	-5.9	100.0	35.5	20.0	0.16	0.09	50.3	0.23
Italy	3 430	0.17	-6.9	99.8	74.7	27.9	0.12	0.05	27.9	0.05
Japan	11 582	0.23	2.1	89.1	25.6		0.06		60.4	0.14
Korea	1 755	0.13	16.8	95.1	25.4		0.03		40.5	0.05
Luxembourg	429	1.00	-0.8	100.0	30.4	21.5	0.30	0.22	37.9	0.38
Netherlands	5 435	0.67	-3.1	100.0	32.9	21.0	0.22	0.14	25.1	0.17
New Zealand	457	0.26	1.7	100.0	23.3		0.06		27.6	0.07
Norway	5 581	1.07	2.7	100.0	22.7		0.24		27.6	0.30
Poland	472	0.10	5.5	..	74.4	6.1	0.07	0.01	26.5	0.03
Portugal	488	0.23	0.6	87.7	38.0	5.8	0.09	0.01	29.3	0.07
Slovak Republic	86	0.09	0.2	100.0	81.2	12.1	0.08	0.01	24.3	0.02
Slovenia	62	0.13	-0.1	100.0	66.5	12.7	0.09	0.02	17.5	0.02
Spain	2 375	0.18	-17.2	100.0	60.2	16.7	0.11	0.03	18.9	0.03
Sweden	5 827	1.01	2.2	100.0	32.8	26.4	0.33	0.27	30.9	0.31
Switzerland	3 200	0.45	6.2	100.0	21.7		0.10		25.8	0.12
United Kingdom	17 871	0.70	9.9	100.0	41.3	30.6	0.29	0.22	34.7	0.24
United States	31 497	0.18	3.7	100.0	16.2		0.03		32.4	0.06
Total DAC	**135 072**	**0.30**	**2.0**	**95.1**	**30.8**		**0.09**		**33.0**	**0.10**
Memo: Average country effort		0.39								

Notes:

a. Excluding debt reorganisation.

b. Including EU institutions.

c. Excluding EU institutions.

.. Data not available.

Figure B.I Net ODA from DAC countries in 2013

Per cent of GNI

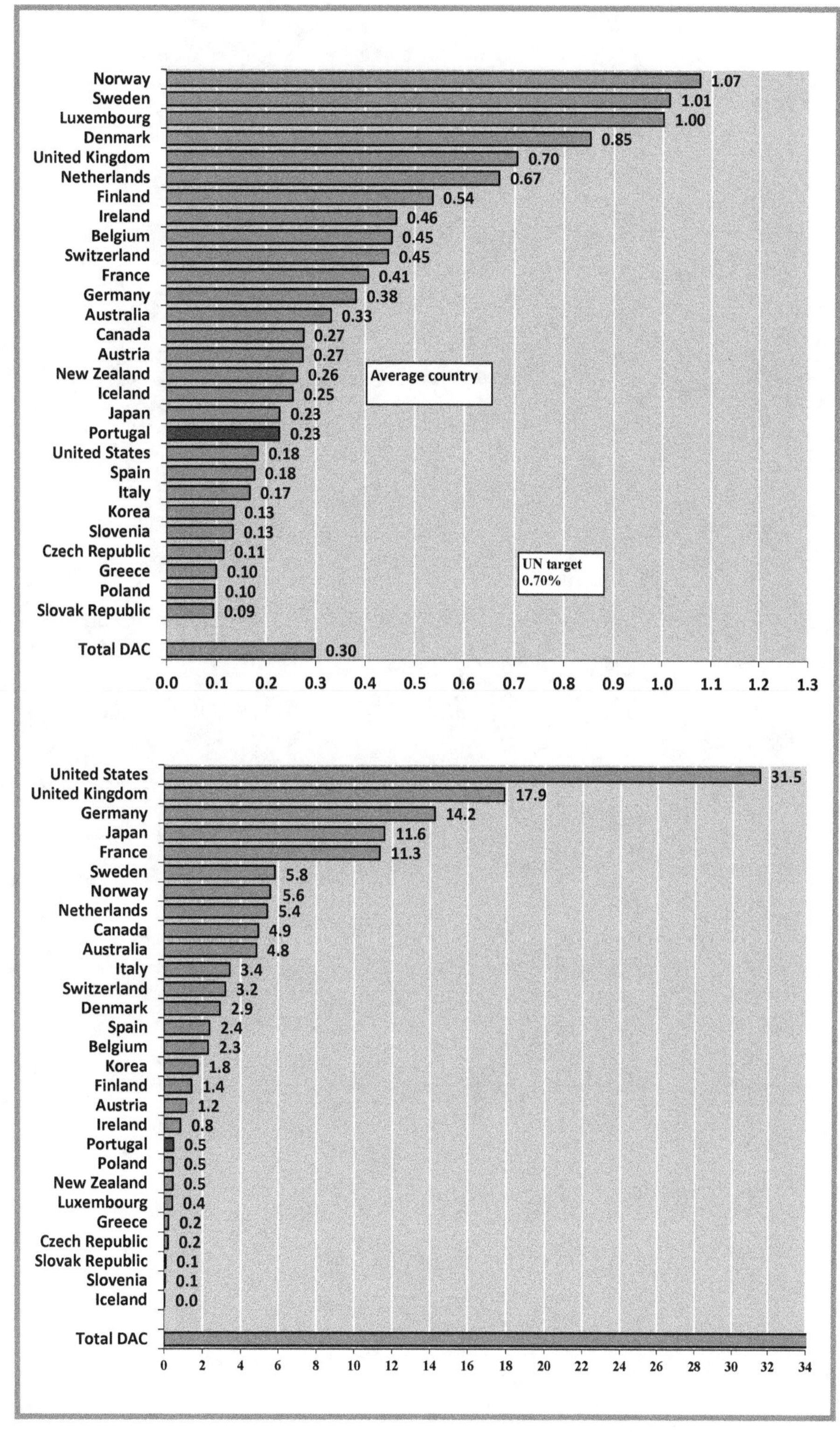

Annex C: Field visit to Sao Tome and Principe

Sao Tome and Principe's Development Context

As part of the peer review of Portugal, a team of examiners from Luxembourg and the Czech Republic, and the OECD Secretariat went to Sao Tome and Principe in May 2015 to gather input from Portuguese development staff and partners. Meetings were held with Portuguese officials in the Embassy, high-level representatives of the government of Sao Tome and Principe, other bilateral donors, multilateral organisations, implementing partners, and representatives of Portuguese and local civil society organisations.

The small island developing state is vulnerable to external shocks

Sao Tome and Principe is an archipelago of just over 1 000 square kilometres situated in the Gulf of Guinea (population 193 000). It is one of the smallest economies in Africa, with a gross domestic product (GDP) of USD 310 million in 2013 (World Bank, 2015). Ranked as a lower-middle income country, the economy is currently dependent on the cocoa sector, although research is being undertaken into the commercial viability of its offshore oil reserves.

Holding its first multiparty elections in 1991, Sao Tome and Principe has been largely free from conflict and violence. However, internal political disputes have caused repeated changes in government, including two failed coups in 1995 and 2003. For a country used to being ruled by fragile coalitions, the current government's absolute majority in parliament is unusual and may provide some much-needed stability.

The Government of Sao Tome and Principe's second poverty reduction strategy paper (2012-2016) promotes good governance, sustainable and inclusive economic growth and social sector improvements (Government of Sao Tome and Principe, 2012). Despite registering significant improvements in human development, Sao Tome and Principe is still classified as a least developed country and a small island developing state by the United Nations. This reflects its vulnerability to external and domestic shocks, particularly climate change. It has made great strides in education and health, but less in reducing poverty: 43.5% of the population was living on less than USD 1.25 a day in 2010.

Portugal is the largest of the few donors supporting the country

Sao Tome and Principe received a total of USD 51.8 million in ODA in 2013. Portugal is by far the country's largest donor, providing USD 19.3 million of ODA in 2013 or 30% of the total. The EU Institutions are the second biggest donor, followed by the World Bank, African Development Bank and Japan (Figure C.1). Non-DAC donors, including Brazil and Taiwan, also provide ODA-like flows to the country.

Portugal's ODA programme focuses on good governance and sustainable development

Sao Tome and Principe is the 5th largest recipient of Portugal's bilateral ODA (2012/13) and is an important partner for Portugal. Portugal's Indicative Country Programme runs between 2012 and 2015 and has a budget of EUR 43.5 million. The programme focuses on the following areas:

Strategic Axis I (8% of budget): Good governance, participation and democracy

- institutional capacity building – government and civil society
- security and development.

Strategic Axis II (92% of budget): Sustainable development and the fight against poverty

- education and basic services
- institutional capacity building in science and technology
- entrepreneurship and business development
- support in the form of products (i.e. credit lines).

Figure C.1 Sao Tome and Principe's aid at a glance

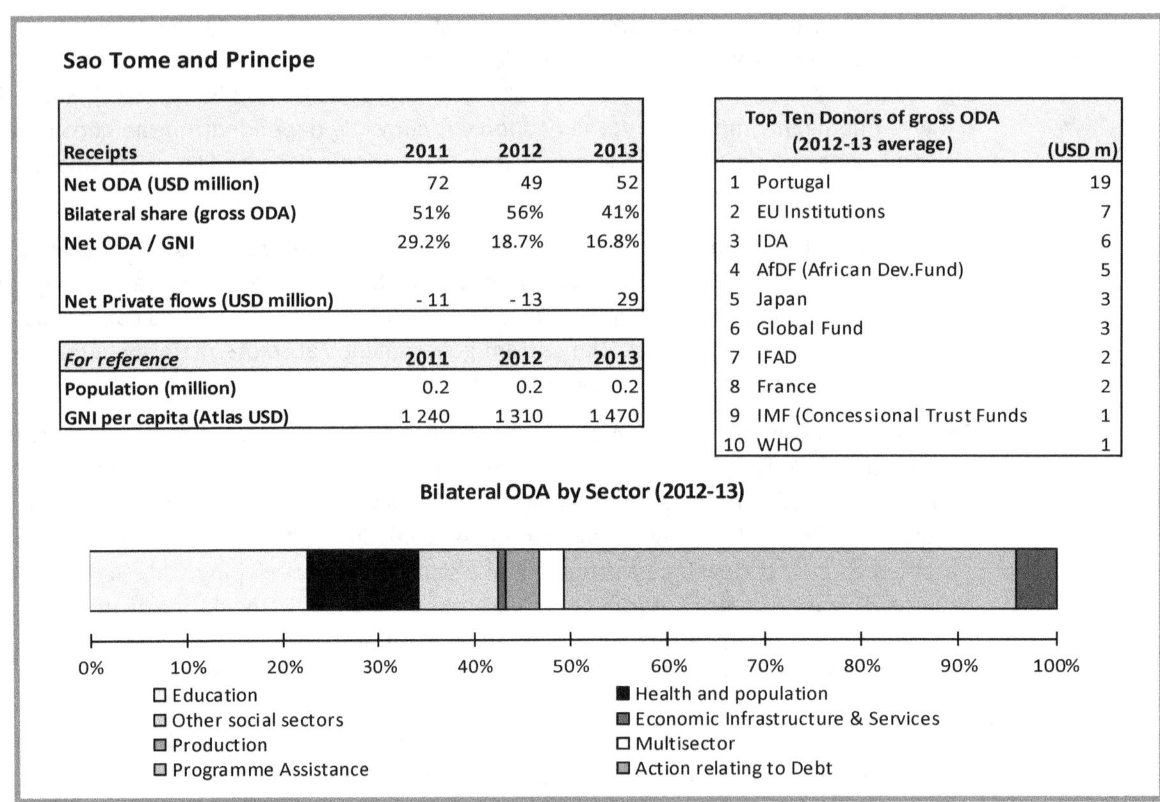

Sao Tome and Principe

Receipts	2011	2012	2013
Net ODA (USD million)	72	49	52
Bilateral share (gross ODA)	51%	56%	41%
Net ODA / GNI	29.2%	18.7%	16.8%
Net Private flows (USD million)	- 11	- 13	29

For reference	2011	2012	2013
Population (million)	0.2	0.2	0.2
GNI per capita (Atlas USD)	1 240	1 310	1 470

Top Ten Donors of gross ODA (2012-13 average)		(USD m)
1	Portugal	19
2	EU Institutions	7
3	IDA	6
4	AfDF (African Dev.Fund)	5
5	Japan	3
6	Global Fund	3
7	IFAD	2
8	France	2
9	IMF (Concessional Trust Funds	1
10	WHO	1

Source: OECD - DAC, World Bank; www.oecd.org/dac/stats

Portugal's policies, strategies and aid allocation

Portugal is a valued long-term partner

Sao Tome and Principe appreciate Portugal as a long-term, reliable and responsive partner. The shared language and extensive cultural and historical ties between the two countries have fostered a strong relationship that goes well beyond development co-operation.

Strong commitment to ownership

Portugal remains highly committed to the principle of ownership. The Government of Sao Tome and Principe is involved in the design, monitoring and evaluation of Portugal's Indicative Cooperation Programme, which as a result is strongly aligned to national policies. The peer review team did note that there can be a tension between adhering to the principle of country ownership and ensuring a consolidated programme, however. Portugal, as the largest donor in the country, is often the first line of request for the government on development matters. As a responsive partner Portugal can, as a result, get pulled into a number of different areas which can lead to a fragmented programme.

The approach to development is comprehensive

Portugal has a strong whole-of-government presence in the country, including representatives from the Ministry of Defence and Interior Affairs and there is regular dialogue between all of Portugal's government actors in the country. As a result, Portugal has been able to deliver a comprehensive development approach – one which goes beyond ODA (Box C.1).

Box C.1 A comprehensive approach to development

Portugal has a comprehensive approach to development in Sao Tome and Principe which goes beyond ODA. Its currency stabilisation agreement with the country, which is guaranteed by the Portuguese Central Bank and the Ministry of Finance, ensures Sao Tome and Principe's Dobra is pegged to the Euro. This has fostered macro-economic stability and helped to bring down high inflation rates. Its maritime security agreement with the country involves the Portuguese military providing regular surveillance of the territorial waters of Sao Tome and Principe. This is intended to preserve national and regional security and resources from human and drug trafficking and illegal fishing.

Source: Interviews undertaken during the field mission.

Good sector concentration, though still many small projects

While Portugal's ODA is relatively concentrated at the sector level in Sao Tome and Principe, it still continues to have a significant number of small activities. This is due, in part, to the numerous Portuguese development actors delivering ODA and the limited number of other donors in the country. In 2013 it had 56 activities being undertaken (excluding those related to concessional loans) under its USD 10.7 million grant programme with the country. Over half of these (39) were under USD 100 000. The management of so many activities imposes transaction costs on all parties and hinders Portugal's ability to achieve greater focus and economies of scale.

Cross-cutting issues are not yet well integrated into programming

Portugal is starting to take account of its cross-cutting issues of gender equality and the environment and climate change in its flagship programmes in Sao Tome and Principe. Nonetheless, limited guidance from headquarters and the lack of a focal point at the Embassy to support staff and implementing partners makes it difficult for Portugal to ensure these issues are systematically mainstreamed across all its programmes.

In 2013, 38% of Portugal's ODA to the country was targeted at gender equality and woman's empowerment (USD 6.63 million). In contrast, only 2% of its ODA (USD 430 000) targeted at environment-related objectives. Given that Sao Tome and Principe is a small island developing state and particularly vulnerable to the impacts of climate change, there is scope for Portugal to increase its current environment-related ODA to the country that is focused on tackling climate change and is co-ordinated with the UN.

Organisation and management

Greater engagement of staff in the programme, but scope for more delegated authority

Portugal's drive to increase numbers of and delegate authority to staff in the field is evident in Sao Tome and Principe. The Embassy has seven staff working on development co-operation, along with the Ambassador. They were all engaged in organising the evaluation of the current country programme and starting consultations for the new programme. They felt that headquarters listened to them.

However, the exact division of responsibilities between the field and headquarters was not always clear to the peer review team. There is scope for Portugal to clarify this. In addition, despite progress, more financial and programming authority could be delegated. The peer team was informed that the Embassy in Sao Tome and Principe only had financial authority over a EUR 10 000 local governance fund. All other financial decisions were taken at headquarters. The development co-operation staff working in the Embassy could play a more leading role in the design of the new Strategic Cooperation Programme and in the programme management cycle. This should include those co-operation staff representing other line ministries. This would increase efficiency and help ensure strategies and programmes are more context-specific, build on knowledge of local institutional constraints and risks, and draw on experience.

Local staff are under-used

At the time of the peer review mission there were no local staff working exclusively on development co-operation in the Embassy. Given human resource constraints in headquarters Portugal could explore how local staff could play a role in development co-operation.

Lack of effective information management system

While information does flow among Portugal, its numerous development actors (within the field, and to and from headquarters) and its partners, it does not always do so in the most efficient manner. Effective communication is undermined by the lack of clear and simple reporting lines and a modern and comprehensive information management system accessible to all Portuguese development actors.

Partnerships, results and accountability

Joint evaluations are good practice

At the time of the peer review mission, Portugal and Sao Tome and Principe were embarking on a joint evaluation of Portugal's Indicative Cooperation Programme which comes to an end in 2015. The findings of this evaluation will be used to develop the new Strategic Cooperation Programme. This is good practice, enabling partner countries to voice praise and criticism of Portugal's performance.

Country systems are not yet used

The vast majority of Portugal's ODA to the country is provided as projects; none of the grant ODA uses partner country's public finance management systems. As the country develops, Portugal should seek to find opportunities to use a wider variety of aid modalities and make greater use of country systems in conjunction with other donors.

Results measured at project level, but not yet at the country programme level	Portugal is identifying and monitoring project results in Sao Tome and Principe, but so far only outputs are measured, and not outcomes. Country-level results are not yet being identified or monitored. The new Strategic Cooperation Programme will be an opportunity to rectify this. Setting out measurable objectives for Portugal's entire country programme and regularly measuring progress towards them will enable Portugal to better assess its overall performance in the country.
Portugal supports local civil society, but funding mechanisms are cumbersome and dialogue limited	Portugal supports civil society in Sao Tome and Principe, providing USD 3.6 million in ODA to local and Portuguese civil society organisations in 2013. However, Portuguese NGOs confirmed the peer review team's impression in Lisbon that Camões I.P. could streamline its approach to funding civil society organisations. Portuguese NGOs highlighted the high transactions costs they face, relative to other donors, in accessing funding from the institute. Portuguese NGOs in Sao Tome and Principe also called for more regular dialogue with the Embassy to enable them to have input into the new country strategy, to share information on activities and foster greater co-ordination in the field.

Bibliography

Government sources

IPAD (2012), *Evaluation of Sao Tome and Principe's Indicative Co-operation Programme (2008-11)*, *Instituto Português de Apoio ao Desenvolvimento*, Lisbon.

MNE/IPAD (2012), *Indicative Co-operation Programme for Sao Tome and Principe 2012-15*, *Ministério dos Negócios Estrangeiros* and IPAD, Lisbon.

Other sources

Government of Sao Tome and Principe (2012), *Second Poverty Reduction Strategy Paper (PRSPII)*, Government of Sao Tome and Principe.

World Bank (2015), *Overview of Sao Tome and Principe Development Context*, The World Bank, Washington DC, www.worldbank.org/en/country/saotome/overview.

Annex D: Portugal's credit lines 2001-14

Table D.1 Portugal's credit lines 2001-14

As of 31/12/2014

Date	Country		CRS ID	Description	Total Amount of the Line of Credit (EUR)	Interest rate (%)	Amount committed to specific loans / projects (EUR)	Amount disbursed (EUR)
01-05-2001	136	Morocco	2001009014	Line of credit for import support to SME's	10,000,000	0.750	1,765,000	1,765,000
26-11-2004	136	Morocco	2004009005	Line of credit for capital goods and services	200,000,000	3.340	124,494,000	124,494,000
24-11-2007	230	Cabo Verde	2007009001	Line of credit for capital goods and services	200,000,000	1.580	184,698,000	184,698,000
17-07-2008	225	Angola	2008009028	Line of credit for capital goods and services	100,000,000	1.890	30,039,000	30,039,000
01-07-2008	259	Mozambique	2008009029	Line of credit for capital goods and services	400,000,000	1.890	351,489,000	351,489,000
20-05-2008	730	China	2008009030	Line of credit for capital goods and services	300,000,000	3.274	26,787,000	26,787,000
29-06-2009	230	Cabo Verde	2009008912	Line of credit for renewable energy projects	100,000,000	1.710	76,246,000	76,246,000
25-02-2009	268	São Tomé Pr.	2009008844	Line of credit for capital goods and services	50,000,000	1.890	28,094,000	28,094,000
29-01-2011	230	Cabo Verde	2011009000	Line of credit for social housing	200,000,000	1.710	108,998,000	108,998,000
24-01-2014	230	Cabo Verde	2014009000	Expansion and modernization of the Port of Sal-Rei	30,000,000	1.370	25,350,000	25,350,000

Source: Government of Portugal (2015).

ORGANISATION FOR ECONOMIC CO-OPERATION AND DEVELOPMENT

The OECD is a unique forum where governments work together to address the economic, social and environmental challenges of globalisation. The OECD is also at the forefront of efforts to understand and to help governments respond to new developments and concerns, such as corporate governance, the information economy and the challenges of an ageing population. The Organisation provides a setting where governments can compare policy experiences, seek answers to common problems, identify good practice and work to co-ordinate domestic and international policies.

The OECD member countries are: Australia, Austria, Belgium, Canada, Chile, the Czech Republic, Denmark, Estonia, Finland, France, Germany, Greece, Hungary, Iceland, Ireland, Israel, Italy, Japan, Korea, Luxembourg, Mexico, the Netherlands, New Zealand, Norway, Poland, Portugal, the Slovak Republic, Slovenia, Spain, Sweden, Switzerland, Turkey, the United Kingdom and the United States. The European Union takes part in the work of the OECD.

OECD Publishing disseminates widely the results of the Organisation's statistics gathering and research on economic, social and environmental issues, as well as the conventions, guidelines and standards agreed by its members.

DEVELOPMENT ASSISTANCE COMMITTEE

To achieve its aims, the OECD has set up a number of specialised committees. One of these is the Development Assistance Committee (DAC), whose mandate is to promote development co-operation and other policies so as to contribute to sustainable development - including pro-poor economic growth, poverty reduction and the improvement of living standards in developing countries - and to a future in which no country will depend on aid. To this end, the DAC has grouped the world's main donors, defining and monitoring global standards in key areas of development.

The members of the DAC are Australia, Austria, Belgium, Canada, the Czech Republic, Denmark, the European Union, Finland, France, Germany, Greece, Iceland, Ireland, Italy, Japan, Korea, Luxembourg, the Netherlands, New Zealand, Norway, Poland, Portugal, the Slovak Republic, Slovenia, Spain, Sweden, Switzerland, the United Kingdom and the United States.

The DAC issues guidelines and reference documents in the DAC Guidelines and Reference Series to inform and assist members in the conduct of their development co-operation programmes.

OECD PUBLISHING, 2, rue André-Pascal, 75775 PARIS CEDEX 16
(43 2015 10 1 P) ISBN 978-92-64-24856-4 – 2015

www.ingramcontent.com/pod-product-compliance
Lightning Source LLC
LaVergne TN
LVHW080929120826
845149LV00018B/1746

* 9 7 8 9 2 6 4 2 4 8 5 6 4 *